My Soul Told On Me

Where Pain Meets Power

My Soul Told On Me

She Carries

Chántelle Adanna Agbro

iUniverse®

MY SOUL TOLD ON ME
SHE CARRIES

KJV
Scripture quotations marked KJV are from the Holy Bible, King James Version (Authorized Version). First published in 1611. Quoted from the KJV Classic Reference Bible, Copyright © 1983 by The Zondervan Corporation.

iUniverse books may be ordered through booksellers or by contacting:

iUniverse
1663 Liberty Drive
Bloomington, IN 47403
www.iuniverse.com
1-800-Authors (1-800-288-4677)

ISBN: 978-1-5320-5883-7 (sc)
ISBN: 978-1-5320-5884-4 (e)

Library of Congress Control Number: 2019942647

Print information available on the last page.

iUniverse rev. date: 05/17/2019

foreword

We all have a close circle of friends. Within this circle, the degrees of friendship vary and each relationship serves a defined purpose in your life. There's the blunt friend who always tells it like it is, the wise friend, who's sensible beyond their years, the loyal friend, who you know will be there forever, and the confidant that you run for any and everything. In the years that I have known Chantelle, I've watched her grow to embody all of these friend types. She's passionate, confident and lives without fear of the future. She blossoms because she understands her journey can't be affected by the thoughts and opinions of others. She learns from her experiences and crafts the life that she envisions for herself. She lives unapologetically in her skin, her truth.

In today's society, instant gratification consumes us. As a whole, we fail to understand that nothing is instantaneous. We forget that anything worth having is worth waiting for. We have destination addiction and set our eyes on a goal without understanding the process it takes to arrive there. This memoir seizes those moments and captures the journey first-hand. As you turn these pages, take a second to reflect and remember... nothing in life comes easy. It takes time to realize your passion, growth to discern your purpose, practice to understand that not everyone and everything is good for you, patience to learn that your current situation is not your final destination, and faith to manifest your destiny. As Theodore Roosevelt once said, "Nothing in the world is worth having or worth doing unless it means effort, pain, difficulty... I have never in my life envied a human being who led an easy life. I have envied a great many people who led difficult lives and led them well."

This memoir invites you to see Chantelle in her most vulnerable state. Her words allow you to travel along with her on this self-reflective journey towards mastering peace. As you read this memoir, realize that these stories come from a place of growth. Her words share stories of learning and accepting what many of us are unable to do - embrace our flaws. Each poem, story and prose narrates the importance of finding, owning and living in one's truth. If there's anyone who is walking representation of self-reflection, it's Chantelle. She and I couldn't live more different lives, but I can relate so well to her journey and I'm sure you will able to, too.

Indera

Preface

My soul is the one and only entity that has lived through every emotional, physical, and mental encounter I've endured. It has heard and nurtured the sound-aches and beats of my heart. It has always found the strength, courage, and durability to somehow keep me here, whether I'm groaning, growing, or glowing. It's kept me here, kept me present in ways and on days I wanted to be permanently absent. I hoarded pain, doubt, insecurity, secrets, lies, and anger in me. I bottled it all and wore the many destructive masks of pride, ego, confusion, and—most of all—fear. It's safe to say that my place of paradise and peace was demolished because I let it be so.

My mind was invaded.

My clear sight faded.

Faded, until it was nonexistent.

Only was it then, when I'd been covered by complete darkness, that I began to love myself. I had no choice but to show up for myself, no choice but to turn to myself for the help I previously sought from someone else. That pressure-that isolation from everyone and everything forced me to meticulously listen to myself. I had to dig deep inside, passed the point where most people run and hide, and that's where I found my light.

Weird, the irony of one extreme birthing the other.

But it did, and it did it with all its might.

Nevertheless, my soul began to do, feel, act, and be something that unfortunately seemed foreign. It reverted to its natural desire for pure joy, comfort, peace, and openness. It started to search for a different type of energy, the kind where love and peace create an unbreakable synergy.

Again, I was love; I was my own vicious addiction, and I craved that fix daily. I sought everything—everyone good and whole and full of sun.

It all was mine.

This powerful feeling of light kept trying to creep and seep its way through my dark, secluded cracks of insecurities, numbness, and exhaustion and again hoarded pain.

But it couldn't.

It was not able to form, to be, to reach its maximum potential because, per usual, I let fear get the best of me.

I kept blocking and limiting, every chance I got. I was in my own way. I contained my truth; I suppressed it, and I resisted it, over and over and over again, for as long as I could, until the moment my soul finally had enough.

I was fed up with myself.

I had reached the point in my life where this relentless and amorous feeling outweighed any fear that could ever exist, and it firmly took hold.

Right then. Right there.

My soul told on me.

It told you, me, and anyone else affected by my untamed sea.

It said,

I can't do this anymore. I love you. I love you more than you'll ever know. I'm here to love, so let's do what we came to do. I choose you because you are you, not for what others can't do or what they fail to see in you. I can't continue to hold you hostage. There is so much more to you than this parasitic disease of bitterness that you're letting consume you. Oppose this grim image you've chosen to show. I can no longer be the holding cell for all you've managed to keep pent up.

Aggression. Disappointment. Sadness. Self-doubt. Self-hate.

Baby-love,

Let. That. Shit. Go.

Set yourself apart. Set me free. Set us free. And let it go.

Now, inhale, exhale, and realign.

Speak up in this moment, claim this liberating space, and call it your peace place.

Your time is now.

Introduction

Hey, hey, hey!

Welcome, my loves, and thank you so much for taking time to know me in *My Soul Told On Me.*

You're probably wondering why you'd want to read more than 50, one hundred or even two hundred pages about my soul telling on me, huh? And what does that even mean?

Well, there's no doubt that you're already intrigued. Whether you caught it or not, your subconscious lured you my way, and I'm going to make sure my story is so soul-filling that you'll not only want to stay but beg for more when we're finally through.

From the looks of it, I am no one for you to concern yourself with. No one for you to feel deeply over—that is, not until I give you a reason to.

We will learn so much together, but this isn't just about me. It's about my journey and helping you to see how that reflects who you choose to be.

And I hope you choose … free.

People are mirrors. They often reflect to others what they are themselves.

I will do my best to mirror you, to speak on what is often thought but rarely voiced, while giving you exclusives on the misunderstood mystery of "Telley" (my nickname).

This will be a life-changing conversation, and we have loads to cover, so let's get to it.

CHAPTER 1

It's Only the Beginning

Contrary to what some might think, I am an open-minded and ambitious young woman with the utmost love to give.

Exploring and navigating through my twenties is definitely something … interesting.

I've come across a lot of confusion and scattered puzzle pieces in this game, which constantly has me questioning if I was ever supposed to be sane.

Kidding—not kidding.

I'm wise enough to know that I'm far from having it all figured out, but I've decided to articulate my tsunami of a life for you up until this point.

In this piece, my peace of art, I'll share agony, tears, laughter, joy, and epiphanies from every angle. This confession has shaped me; it shaped me for me and then for you.

Transparency.

You should feel lucky because whether you're dealing with the great things, sad things, replenishing things, confusing things, or unexplainable things, it is all *connected*.

We are all connected … and you're not alone.

I'm right here, going through it with you on some level. I hope that all I unravel will be useful and inspiring to you but, most important, that it will be soul food for you.

I have grown *a lot.*

Let me say that again—*I have grown a lot.* And I thank GOD that I'm still growing.

I've had the privilege of being exposed to real and genuine people with contagious energy, and let me tell you, that's the purest and most unworldly feeling. It's important that I write my feelings as vividly as I know how, as I experience them.

Because what I feel, what you feel, what we feel is not irrelevant, is not shameful, and is not inadequate. It's relevant and rich with respect to bonds and human interactions that we have with others but especially with ourselves.

While reading and familiarizing yourself with the layers of my soul, I don't want you to make comparisons. I don't want you to dwell on the differences or the similarities but on everything in between.

Try to focus on what's real, what you feel, and what you can't quite name, but you know it keeps you sane.

In a time where we are constantly pressured to highlight the major differences with negative connotations, I challenge you to do exactly the opposite with a little twist.

Millennials and younger generations are often "lost," but I think that's because of miscommunication and misunderstanding. Despite the reasoning, however, I have a duty to insightfully learn and then intentionally live, to become inspired and then inspire, to become creative and then create.

Life, up until this point, has humbled me. I know that many individuals have had more challenging obstacles than I've had, but that doesn't take away from my pain, from what I dealt with. I want to tell you that I sincerely care about you, and you have a purpose in this life, and that purpose is to love, if nothing else.

Love is not tangible.

Love is deeper than words.

Love is deeper than the ocean's floor and then some.

Love is deeper than sound, light, space, time.

Love is deeper than anything physical and is the core of everything intangible.

It can be recognized through the smallest of actions.

Love *carries* much weight.

We are all so intensely intertwined with and interrelated to one another—as beings, as energies, and as vibrations riding through similar frequencies—that it devastates me how detached we can be. We are severely divided by none other than *ignorance* and it pains me.

> Nothing in all the world is more dangerous than
> sincere ignorance and conscientious stupidity.
>
> —Martin Luther King Jr.

Whether it's division by race, class, gender, sexual orientation, religion, or colorism, you name it, and it just shouldn't be.

But what do I know? I'm just a black girl in her early twenties, discovering the world inch by inch, unpacking that "black-girl magic" one sparkle at a time.

I do know that our similarities are far greater than our distinctions.

We all bleed blood.

We all occupy the same earth.

Before we get into the meat of things, let me thank you for taking a chance on me. If you embrace creative mindfulness and authenticity in its rawest and rarest form, then you will love everything about me and my work of art.

This exclusive look into my beautiful, artistic, but sometimes chaotic mind is still new but very dear to me, yet the timing couldn't have been more perfect.

Even though I'm sharing it with the world, you will relate only as far as you have come yourself.

You will run your intimate race at your own pace.

There are aspects in this book that I've never told anyone, so consider yourself pure gold, not just because I've included you in on the details of my heart's treasures but because it will help you become more in tune with yourself and with your treasures, as well.

You have a front row seat to a lucid and fluid understanding of who I am as a person.

You, my friend, are very special, and I appreciate you.

CHAPTER 2

Beautifully Misunderstood

Don't you love it when you get the condescending questions or sly remarks such as:

"You're such a bitch!"

"That's why no one likes you."

"Why are you so bitter?"

"Why are you so angry all the time? What's wrong with you?"

"You're boring."

"You're too difficult!"

"You're just too much!"

But wait—these are my favorites:

"Oh, now I see why you're single."

"You're a spoiled brat!"

"You're never going to find love with that attitude."

"You are crazy! How do people even deal with you?"

This list could go on.

I've personally heard similar comments from individuals who don't even know me, let alone understand me, but who have "concern" for me and the way I live my life, including one that certainty got under my skin: "Chántelle, you're rich." People said that to me in elementary and middle school and throughout high school and sometimes still do in my adult life.

It makes me question people's true intentions with me when they focus on what I have. When people have told me that I'm rich, it was with the implication that everything was handed to me; that I had no right to feel the way I felt about certain things; that I never needed to worry about anything; and that I didn't know what the word *struggle* meant.

My biggest problem with this comment is that they *assumed*. People thought (and still do think) they had me figured out as a person—how I should feel, how I should live my life, what I should be grateful for, etc.

That wasn't okay at all.

The first time people said this to me or made slick comments that suggested any of the statements above, I thought, *Okay, I understand that to some people, looking solely at material possessions, it may seem as though I am "rich."* Yet that's not the case at all, and I don't present myself as better than anyone, so why do people want to treat me like I do?

I can admit that I'm "rich" in a different sense. I'm rich because my sister and I never had to want for anything. We have been fortunate enough, by the grace of God, to not just survive but enjoy life.

I am not saying this to brag. That's just not my character; I'm humble. It's important to realize that appearance is not everything.

For those who do have to hustle, I respect you to no end. You are working with what was dealt to you, and you can and will make it. The key is to find out what works for you, and run with it.

Hustling is not necessarily a bad quality. Sometimes transitioning from short-term grinding to long-term grinding is a challenge, but the truth is people can get lost in anything, and too much of anything isn't beneficial.

I'm currently learning how to hustle. It's a little later in the game for me, but my journey is different from yours—and that's okay.

Everything is about perspective. For example, if your living enviorment is in an urban area, it's more likely for you to have to grow independent faster, generally speaking. Usually, those survival skills come into play quicker because of your pre-mature exposure to life.

I was sheltered, and I hated it. I always wanted to do simple things, like ride the train or the bus, walk to the store alone, or maybe stay home alone once in a while, but it never happened. I thought it was cool to be independent and not have your parents breathing down your neck, twenty-four/seven. But I felt like my mom and dad never let me do anything. In reality, it wasn't that; it was more that they just didn't let me do *everything*.

I did have more freedom in high school, but even then, it didn't seem to be as much freedom as others had.

I often told others, "I wish my parents didn't care about me, because they always want to know what I'm doing, who I'm with, and how long I plan to be out. It's annoying. Plus, my dad asks entirely too many *questions*!"

The response I got from most, which shocked, me, was, "No, Chántelle, you don't wish that. I wish my parents cared more."

At the time, I didn't understand that response, but I do now. I understand that having no other choice but to grow up at a young age can be shattering.

I don't personally know that struggle, but I respect those who did what they had to do to survive and become whole, despite that negligence.

However, just because my parents worked hard so my sister and I wouldn't face that struggle doesn't mean that we didn't see hard times and I need that to be clear. I still sensed when my parents worried about finances and things of that nature. I wasn't in this life, unaware. Just like any other middle-class family, we could portray being better off than we were. Our family situation was not everyone's business, and we knew that God would provide. We also knew that there always were people who were worse off than we were, so we couldn't be comfortable with constantly complaining.

All we can do is pray, take it one day at a time, and thank God for making a way out of no way.

My response to people's ignorance of my situation, however, has been to tell them, "I'm not rich; I'm blessed. If I were rich, my mom wouldn't be slaving for a company that ultimately could care less about her and high quality of work and experience just to let her go. If I were rich, my father, as a small business owner, wouldn't have to battle these prideful, egotistical, racist white men in his field of work to get paid. Or better yet, he wouldn't have to fight and stress over finding more work after being told he won't be paid for thousands of dollars' worth of hard-earned work. Everything is not what it seems folks. Stop trying to make it seem like I'm somehow better than you when I am not, and I don't care to be."

Because I am me and you are you for a reason.

People often didn't realize the effort it took to get my family where it was in life. This lack of understanding wasn't just from friends but even family members, which I will never comprehend. We could be at our lowest, and family would still try to kick us when we were down and asked for handouts. They never once genuinely asked if we needed anything because they assumed we had it all together.

Even now, when it seems we've conquered a very hard time, another one comes along. Things still aren't where they need to be, but they are slowly getting better.

Struggling. Fighting. Surviving. They are still realities for us in one way or another, but no one ever explicitly sees this.

No one knows if we were one missed payment away from losing everything.

Moral of the story: don't be shallow. don't assume. check on the strong ones.

Trust me when I say, I *will* be successful because I know what my parents had to go through to make sure they could always take care of my sister and me. I would be doing a disservice to them, myself, and my future children if my intention to persevere were selfish.

As I've gotten older and wiser, it does something to me, emotionally and mentally, when I see my parents struggle, get tired, and go through the motions each day.

I don't think that is how life is supposed to be lived. So I'm going to be the one to change it for them.

It's all for them and my fallen angels.

So being rich? Well, we are all rich in our own ways.

The only way I see myself being rich is through loving—having a loving family, having a few loving friends—and acquiring the knowledge to realize that God is intentional in everything he does.

I can't help what God chose to give me, but I can help what I choose to do with it, and I choose to spread more love the best way I know how.

It's okay if you don't understand the way my family and I move because not everything is meant to be understood by everybody.

But you **will** respect it.

Some people get defensive and guarded when they are presented with the unknown or when they don't understand something or someone— that's natural. If that's you, challenge yourself to be more open to new opportunities and ideaologies. If that's not your personality, that's cool too; just realize that and keep your distance.

Don't try to keep people closed-minded like you.

We fear what we don't understand. We belittle it. We shy away from it.

Does this resistance keep us safe?

Does it make us any wiser?

Or does it mentally cripple us, making us oblivious to the truth that we are our own worst enemy?

Why is that?

I think it's because we can't make sense of it. Our mental models can't relate "it" to what we already are familiar with, which creates a panic in us. This frightens us so much that we disregard and block our blessings in life, whether consciously or unconsciously.

I am guilty of this!

Quick clarification: to know *of* me (or anyone) is not to *know* me (or anyone). Make sure that your comments or concerns are based on facts and not the "he said/she said" bullshit before you make negative assumptions about people.

Get to know the real *me* first, and then run your mouth, and make sure you always end with, "Yeah, she's doing her thing, though."

I do not **like** to be rude, but when people don't know any better, that sometimes calls for me to step out of character a bit.

You feel me?

Most people don't know that I am *extremely* sensitive. However, I will mask my sensitivity all day, every day, if I must, to avoid being taken advantage of; people are ruthless.

It's a dog-eat-dog world, right?

To be honest, if this were about three years ago, all those comments from other people that I mentioned at the beginning of this chapter would have made me react in one of two ways:

1. I would have shied away from others because it would've gotten under my skin and increased my feelings of insecurity and low self-esteem (*which is what they want*).

2. I would have retaliated by lashing out, having a major attitude, or emotionally and mentally shutting down.

But that was then, and this is now.

Even when I can laugh at these comments, I'm still reminded to never take myself to a place where I become so worked up over situations/opinions/words that I can't change.

Fact: Everyone is entitled to his or her opinion.

Myth: Their opinions shape who I am (my character) and what I decide to associate myself with (my atmosphere).

My epiphany came when I learned that my world is controlled by *me* and *only me*, including every gesture, feeling, reaction, motion, and emotion.

Daily note to self: Nothing and no one can alter who you truly are. It's important to know yourself and know your worth.

I need to build on my character and ignore the rest to stay level-headed through all the misconceptions of me that people have.

I've recognized that folks will choose to keep reading me wrong, no matter what, but that doesn't mean I have to deal with things that constantly bring me down or their corrupt mind-sets.

> There are things that I'm meant to do even if
> they aren't immediately understood.
>
> They sleeping, they sleeping, they sleeping, they sleeping on me
>
> But I don't waste my time tryna prove that I'm something to see, oh
> The real ones they know and the ones that do not I don't need.

—Kehlani

Message to anyone who has ever had any confusion on who I am. It's been a long time comin', but I'm here to tell you that I am the Queen; and I'm fully owning all of what that title means.

> I understood myself only after I destroyed myself. And only in
> the process of fixing myself, did I know who I really was.

—Sade Andria Zabala

Settling never will be an option. I am now, more than ever, mindful of that fact.

I won't settle in any of these:

- Friends/friendships

- Family

- Romantic relationships

- Peace of mind **

It's just that simple.

That's to preserve my sanity, my mental state. I need my inner self to be alive and well, to feed my soul, and that can't be compromised. That's never up for discussion.

I've heard it said, "Only a king can attract a queen, and only a queen can keep a king focused."

But what happens before we even get to the attraction part?

Are kings and queens even being raised these days?

I think Kendrick Lamar said it best: "Got loyalty, got royalty inside my DNA."

But let's be clear: just because royalty is in us by default by being African (black) doesn't mean it's always manifested to its potential.

In fact, it's often not, and the more the counterproductive cycle continues to spiral within us as a people, the more the self-respect, self-value, and self-love will continue to diminish, specifically in minority communities.

These characteristics can only be instilled through education. It's the one and only priority and necessity (yes, above money).

I'll refrain from diving deep into this topic, but I will say that people of color are all *beautifully misunderstood*.

The lack of guidance and care has become more prominent and devastating to our future.

Too many young men are steered the wrong way by kids trapped in adult bodies.

For instance, if your "OG" or "big homie" is not teaching you to love a woman, get money legally, and be self-sufficient as a man, then stop looking up to him. He's not your inspiration. He's just a *child* who's older than you and who missed the same core values in life as he is subjecting you to.

Let that marinate.

Selling ourselves short and settling for less has disgustingly become a major factor in our modern lives, and it rips us of the power that is in us—it's a recurring broken cycle.

This ignorance does great damage and affects an entire race as it reflects the lack of value, respect, love, and appreciation we have for ourselves, let alone for women and especially black women. It's appalling.

It's imperative that we realize the beauty in *black*—in being soil, in being both priceless and pure.

We queens need you. We are rooting for you, and we are your number-one fans.

Each of us is beautifully misunderstood in life, but I'm rooting for you to continuously exceed life's limits.

Remember: There is no rush. This is not a race. Move at your own pace.

Again, I still learn, grow, and explore. I don't have it all figured out, but I do know, from everything that I have been through, there isn't an answer for everything.

I have faith and patience, and that has taken me a long way. I walk with poise and with my head held high, leaving behind everyone and everything that wants to be left behind.

I've learned to honor anyone's wish of wanting my absence from his or her life, temporary or permanent. It's all about timing.

Whatever left without explanation was in my best interest.

I can't stress enough that there is beauty in not knowing.

If you are lucky enough to attract souls who genuinely accept you, without having to understand every minuscule thing about you, then love and keep them forever.

Those are the keepers and are sent from heaven. Don't let them go.

> The fact that you are willing to say, "I do not understand, and it is fine," is the greatest understanding you could exhibit.
>
> —Wayne Dyer

Despite it all, I keep telling myself, "Continue being that person who no one understands."

When you throw everything off, it makes you stand out by default.

I'm not fazed by the ignorance. I believe in myself—and you should believe in yourself too! I will continue to take risks, be spontaneous, and be comfortable being *me* all the time.

No matter who does or doesn't understand me, or who tries or doesn't try to understand, the bottom line is this:

I will *still* shine. I will *still* stand.

I am a star; how could I not shine?

Remember: Understanding is deeper than knowledge. Many people know you, but very few understand you.

Comprehend what that means, and preserve and protect your treasures.

I am determined that the next steps in my life will consist of everything that satisfies my happiness. I'm genuinely at peace with others, but most important, I'm at peace with myself.

Being misunderstood is why I have to keep going. I'm focusing on everyone's feedback and proving them wrong—one word at a time.

I am a conqueror; I do not accept defeat!

CHAPTER 3

She Carries

A woman is the full circle. Within her is the
power to create, nurture and transform.

—Diane Mariechild

She: any female, woman, young lady, and girl.

Whichever term you prefer, the bottom line is that you are her, and *she* carries a lot.

It's crucial to me that everyone who reads my words will see that I speak in different tones for the different women who make up my being. My tone shows where I am coming from so you can better grasp the morals and values that I convey and how I got to where I am today.

I am interconnected with the intensity that I bring into everything that I do. In the end, you will witness how it relates to my purpose.

"She carries" has become the emblem of life. It speaks to everything I've been through, am going through, and will go through.

From the second I laid to rest one of the only women on this earth with whom I had a genuine, close, open, beautiful, and loving connection, I started to *carry*.

I carried to the point where a lot of days I didn't see the point of life anymore. I went through a very dark stage that I shared with only my heart and soul.

The happiness, comfort, confidence, and peace I'd felt had been ripped away from me, never to return. I just wanted the pain to cease; it was becoming hard to hold in.

Although I never attempted suicide, some days it was so heavily on my mind that it started to eat at me. It not only scared me but also ate away at my physical, mental, and emotional stability—and my existence.

The thought of being with my grandmother in heaven felt ideal right after losing her because I didn't know how I was going to carry on without her.

A little bit about my grandma: Josephine Allen was particular in many ways, but she was very gentle and driven by her love for her family. That's one of the things I admired most about her. She was a God-fearing woman but fearless of man because she knew to whom she belonged. She knew it was possible to reach any height because of who God was and how he works.

"Always try, and always dare to do what has not been done."

My grandma genuinely was nothing short of heaven-sent.

When I think about everything she did for people, I realize it was out of this world. She gave, and gave, and gave, but she never let people walk over her. I never understood how she balance those two extremes, but that is my life goal.

When my sister and I were little, my grandma took in and fed a homeless family—a man and woman and their daughter, who was around my age at the time. She made full meals for them and never let them leave hungry.

When my grandma picked up my sister and me from school some days, we would pick them up as well and take them to her house.

My sister and I were scared the first time we met them; it was so unusual to us, but it became normal eventually.

My parents kept us sheltered. That wasn't a bad thing; they were just being parents, but it affected the way we looked at the real world. My grandma was the pathway against that sheltering. She reminded us that the family she looked after were people just like us. They just happened to be less fortunate than we were, and because she could help, she did. Even when she really couldn't afford to help, she still did. To her, with our common denominator as people, it was only right to lend a helping hand.

She humbled my sister and me, as well as my entire family. She made sure that we didn't look at them or anyone sideways, as if we were better— because we weren't. She instilled in us the trait of always welcoming anyone who was in need with open arms.

If Jesus could do it, then who were we not to do so as well?

I didn't understand that concept until just recently, and it puts everything into perspective.

My grandmother and I were very close, so when she became really sick, it was very hard for me, knowing but not wanting to believe the outcome.

It wasn't that I didn't have faith, but I was young, and I knew what had happened to others who had been diagnosed with breast cancer. I saw only the worst, unfortunately.

I can only imagine how it was for Grandma, seeing her family for the last time at the reunion we had in Florida; this was before we got the word that her cancer had spread. Our reunions were always held from Thursday to Sunday. She was saying goodbye to everyone when all of a sudden, tears started to roll down her cheeks. Right then, I wrapped my arms around her waist, as I always did to comfort her and just to be next to her.

I didn't know why she was crying because she'd never cried before when we left a reunion. Then it dawned on me that she knew this was the last time she would see her family, or maybe she only knew that the stakes were high, and that realization saddened her.

I believe God gives us an epiphany of when it's our time to go. I think Grandma knew, I knew, and the family knew that this was her last reunion.

Around this time, Barack Obama was running for president, and this news did wonders for her. As with many other black parents and grandparents who were old-school, my grandma always stressed the importance of education. She had plenty of time to see how life could affect someone negatively because of skin color, and she knew that education could break barriers.

She was so happy and emotional when President Obama won the election. I wish she could've seen the great things he did and tried to do while in office for eight years; she would have been so proud. I know my grandma was very proud of her vote—that her ballot contributed to his making it into office. It was everything she had ever dreamed of for us, for our people. Even though she passed before his inauguration and didn't get to see him sworn in, she was satisfied, knowing that she had supported what she and many others of her time had thought impossible.

The sicker she got, the more our lives adjusted. My sister, my dad, and I would take her to her chemo appointments, but I hated it because each time she went, she just got weaker and weaker.

It made me start to question what was happening to her. What was cancer, really? How could cells kill people so rapidly and viciously? I just questioned it all.

Chemo became too strong for her to handle, and the cancer grew even more aggressive.

I'd think, *How am I supposed to deal with this when I'm in middle school?* Not to take away from what other middle-schoolers went through, but my confusion and pain were valid.

All I did was sit and listen to what my parents said, which was, "Everything is going to be fine. She is going to get better. She is going to make it."

But is it true? I'd think. *Are they just trying to protect my feelings?*

Eventually, the outcome clearly was going to be the opposite of what they were saying to comfort me. I had eyes. I could see what the disease was doing to her.

I asked myself, *How do I stay sane?*

Although it probably wasn't the best answer, I did what I do best: I held it in.

I shut down.

I carried it all.

Things progressed to the point where my grandma had to go to a nursing home for "recovering patients"; it was located right down the street from her house. My sister and I visited her with my dad after school.

I hated seeing her there.

She always looked so miserable and uncomfortable. For me, walking into any type of hospital or nursing home was just too much; it had death written all over it. I wanted her to have no part of death, obviously.

I felt guilty for leaving her there, like I was automatically sentencing her to her grave, and I carried that too.

My thoughts: *My grandma isn't dying; she's going to beat this. She's my warrior!*

After she'd been in the nursing home for a couple of weeks, an unexpected episode happened. My grandma was rushed to the hospital, where the doctors told us that the cancer had spread to her brain. At this point, her body was so weak and frail that chemo wasn't an option—nor was any treatment, for that matter. She wasn't going to get better from here.

Hospice care was the only choice. The only thing they could do was keep her as comfortable as possible. This is when my grandma came to live with us.

The deterioration of her body was overwhelming for her, and it pained her to even talk.

It was during this most severe time that I realized how much I admired my mother. My mom was still going to work. She'd get up two hours early so she'd have time to take care of my grandma and make sure my sister and I were up for school. It took a toll on her emotionally, mentally, and physically. She didn't know it, but I could see it; I could feel it.

On the night my grandmother passed, I felt an indescribable sadness, weight, and silence in the entire house.

It was close to Christmas, and she was sitting in our big rocking chair in the living room. She had a blanket over her because she was always cold. She had just eaten, and she liked to sit and watch TV, preferably Oprah, while her food digested. She would rock and rock until she fell asleep.

After Grandma dozed off, my mom did one of her periodic checks. She realized Grandma was wheezing and not breathing normally. Her head was tilted to the left side. My mom kept calling her name, but she wouldn't wake up.

My mom's voice grew louder, and I could hear the panic in her voice as she called to Grandma. "Ma, are you okay? Ma? Ma?"

I sensed something was wrong. I walked out of my room, peeking over the balcony to get a closer look.

When I saw my mom rush to call 911, I froze.

The ambulance was now on the way.

All this I watched from the balcony, praying that my grandma would wake up.

When the ambulance arrived, my mom came to my room. I'd returned there because I didn't know what else to do.

I was sitting in my computer chair, facing my door, and the next thing I knew, she came in and said, "We are taking Grandma to the hospital."

I asked, for the last time, "Is she going to be okay?"

My mom was scared but tried to be hopeful. She said, "Yes, everything is going to be okay."

I watched through my tear-filled eyes as the ambulance drive off through, and I knew that was the last time I would see my grandma.

My aunt was in the house, watching my sister and me, and about thirty minutes later, the house phone rang.

I knew I wasn't supposed to pick it up, so I waited for it to stop ringing, indicating that my aunt had answered it. Then I picked up to listen in on the line because I wanted to know what was happening.

I heard my mom say in a shattered voice, "Yeah, we lost her."

I put the phone back on the hook and curled up in a ball on my bed. For the first time—but not the last time—I felt *numb*. It didn't seem real to me at all.

I was so numb that I got on the phone right after that with my boyfriend and talked to him as if nothing had happened. Later that night, however, and into the next morning, it all started to come together, piece by piece, leading up to the day we laid her to rest.

That next morning, my mom and dad called my sister into my room and told us that had passed away the previous night. The doctors couldn't get her heart to recesitate after rushing her to the hospital.

I was quiet; I said absolutely nothing. I just started crying, and I wanted to be alone.

They told us that we didn't have to go to school that day. My state of mind was nonexistent because I felt, but I didn't feel at the same time.

Before Grandma's funeral, my mother asked my sister and me if we had anything to say. I had a lot to say, but if I had to read it in front of everyone, I knew I wouldn't be able to keep it together, so I said no.

"Are you sure?" my mom asked.

Again, I said no.

To this day, I regret not expressing my true feelings. I regret holding it in because I had so many feelings, and my thoughts were so complex that I should've built up the courage to do it for my grandma. She deserved that from me, at least that. I would have done anything for her, and I hope she forgives me for that day, when I wasn't representing how she raised us to be when I decided not to speak.

I'm so glad God can read us without our saying a word because the pain I carried and still carry is indescribable. I couldn't describe it to you, even if I wanted to.

What was I carrying besides pain?

- Answer:

- Sadness

- Confusion

- Hopelessness

- Hatred

- Bitterness

- Discomfort

- Anger

- All of the above (and then some)

All these emotions began to surface from one moment to the next. I spoke to no one about it, and that was the first step of my self-destruction, though I didn't know it yet.

I didn't know how to communicate, and I didn't want to express my feelings to anyone. I thought no one understood me, so I didn't see the point in wasting my time. That was a very lonely place.

Communication just wasn't my thing. I just cried, kept to myself all the time.

In the years after losing my grandmother, I started high school and then college, where I was introduced to even more situations where I felt obligated to *carry*.

The years of being our innocent and carefree selves, for the most part, stop when we enter high school. We begin worrying about things and making decisions that affect the next moves in our lives. It's also a time where our wants come into play, and our biggest decisions shift from which Bratz doll we should play with to how we're going to pay our senior dues.

Then comes the "shit gets real" stage, and we're introduced to college or other options after high school graduation. In college, we must decide on a major or whether we should pledge a sorority. We might ask ourselves how we're going to pay for tuition and books.

But back to my story ...

I was going through many different emotions, and it only became worse in high school.

Myth

- Strong people are immune from being hurt, especially women, because they're used to it.

- I am strong enough to handle pain, so I deserve it.

Fact

- You never know how strong you are until being strong is the only choice you have.

- The strongest people need the most support, comfort, and reassurance that they aren't alone, especially women.

When high school started, everyone referred to me as the "sweetest girl" because I was quiet and shy. I didn't know anyone. Most of the kids came from the local public middle schools, but I was new to the area and had attended a private school (pre-K to eighth grade) in Hyattsville called Concordia Lutheran School.

Of course, I got acquainted with some people, but after a while of my being the sweet, kind, generous, and genuine kid that I was, despite what I was going through emotionally, it just wasn't enough. People wanted more. They saw an opportunity to take advantage of me. (That was the wrong move on their parts, for various reasons.) Others saw an opportunity to cling to me and never let me go. (This, among other things, made me grateful for my family and friends. They were my team and the real MVPs.)

> Nobody likes us except for us, all I ever needed
> was the squad so that's what's up.

—Drake

Others' misconceptions of me were that I was weak. I was a pushover. I couldn't say no.

Again, I started to carry. I didn't know how to address their misconceptions without turning all the way around and becoming a completely unlikeable and bitter person, a *bitch*, so that's exactly what I did.

There was no balance. There was no filter.

What you saw and heard from me was exactly what you received, but to the extreme. And I did not care.

I felt empty. I was cold inside, and I will admit that I became heartless.

There was no in between. I hadn't noticed that about myself yet, so I kept going along, thinking that I was being me and protecting me. But in actuality, I was slowly *losing me.*

I started to then completely shut down.

I didn't know what was what.

I didn't know who was who.

And I really didn't care.

I just carried too much.

Things continued to spiral out of control in my life, and during this time I had low self-esteem issues. I didn't know how to handle it. The decisions I made literally were at the toss of a coin.

This is the challenge with those of us who carry so much and are forced to be strong beyond measure: we get so used to being numb to emotion and feelings that when being strong is too aggressive for a certain circumstance or person, we become poison and are detrimental to not only them, but to our own lives.

There is no "tone down" button. It's scary, and it's difficult as well.

I told myself, "You have to stay strong. You can't let them see you hurt, upset, mad, or lost because that's what they want."

Consequently, my emotions persistently grew out of control, and I kept piling one thing on top of another that I had to carry. It was all harmful, which I knew, but it was my escape and how I managed to cope … for a time. It was like my drug, and I was addicted.

Little did I know that this method was only a temporary fix.

From hanging with the wrong crowd, to lying to my parents about my whereabouts, to engaging in activities and making decisions that were a threat to my morals and beliefs, I had gone a bit too far. I wasn't doing hard-core drugs or having relations with multiple people, but I was being quite rebellious in my own way.

Ugly people, ugly situations, irrational decisions, and dark energies were a part of me. Sadly, nothing that was beautiful, genuine, inspiring, or comforting seemed to be *me* anymore.

People were there one day and gone the next. I lost two close cousins within a year (in the midst of it all).

One of my cousins, Brandon Lee Spruill, was like the older brother I never had, and I just could not take losing him. His sudden, ruthless murder shattered parts in me that I didn't even know were breakable. In turn, I unintentionally hurt people with respect to relationships and family bonds because I was hurting.

I exchanged words with others with no meaning behind them. I made promises (and promises were made to me) that were then broken.

I was quick to shut out my family, close friends, the one pickle-head boy I've ever loved, and anyone else who cared about me, and it was all because I *carried.*

One day after cheerleading practice, my sister innocently came in my room, just to ask me how my day was and to see what I was doing.

Each time she asked me a question, I was very short and irritable in my response. She kept asking, and asking, and asking until I just snapped!

Her last words, while walking out the door, were, "Okay ... what's wrong with you?"

And I just said, "Leave me alone, and leave my room."

I hate myself for that. For not being able to recognize what I was feeling and respectfully channel that energy.

I was extremely messed up inside, and none of it was her or anyone else's fault. I needed help desperately because I was hurting my support system—the people that I would be absolutely nothing without—and that had to end.

But I had no idea how to stop it. How could I stop something that I didn't want talk about? I had all this baggage to carry, and I wouldn't let anyone get close to the root of it, so it stayed there.

Unbothered.

Untouched.

Just waiting for the right moment to permanently destroy me—my potential. My seed. My treasure.

But the devil is a liar:

> Then I will give them a heart to know me, that I am the LORD; and they shall be My people, and I will be their God, for they shall return to me with their whole heart.

> —Jeremiah 24:7

I've come to realize through prayer, patience, and good company that my life, my being, and my presence, has great significance—much more than I've ever given it credit for.

I made a vow then to make better choices that added to my life's unquestionable value. I started referring daily to the golden and essential qualities I possessed in a rhythmic flow:

I am a nurturer.

I am a conqueror.

I am unique.

I am a blessing.

I am a queen.

It took time (and it is still taking time), but it works.

Women birth the world. If you give them anything, they will take it and transform it into something wonderful, useful, and beneficial. Despite all that they carry, they will not self-destruct. They will not be consumed. They will overcome and prevail!

At the right time, the sweet fragrance of a woman's life will fill the room, and she will be irresistible.

God knew what he was doing when he built me.

As women, we carry the seed that blossoms into something breathtaking in every aspect. And just because we carry so much, we deserve so much more!

Are you alluring yet?

CHAPTER 4

Identify the Essentials, and Eliminate the Rest

I am coming for everything they said I couldn't have.

The importance we give to our bodily functions working each day is the same importance we ourselves should acquire with time, as well as every person, every feeling, and every vibe we encounter and put effort into.

Simple gifts like waking up in the morning, inhaling and exhaling, moving each muscle in our bodies and blinking are essential to our existence.

Whoever brings you the most peace should get the most time. It's that simple.

Is every person to whom you give your time and effort essential to you? You may be thinking of individuals who have no significance to your life whatsoever. Yet you still try to justify why you can't cut them off.

At the end of the day, that's your business, but there isn't a good enough justification, ever, to compromise on your peace of mind. Remember that.

Don't be fraudulent with yourself; be true because you're only hindering and harming you.

I am fearless, hungry, and unstoppable in what I desire.

My entire paradigm has shifted pertaining to the people who need to be around in accordance with my elevation. It became apparent to me that if everyone who I claimed was close to me was truly vital to my growth as a person, then I wouldn't have to think twice about it.

I wouldn't have to question intentions or anything else, but I found that I was doing just that, more often than not, and I hated it.

I was keeping people around me who were just using me—for my car, my house, my personality, and my kindness. This was when I was in high school, so maybe the pettiness should have been expected, but who wants to be used? Who wants to find out that people wanted to be friends for all the wrong reasons? They weren't genuinely advocating for my best interests.

Now, I don't necessarily mean that others are using you if you don't physically get something from them, but you should gain intangibles, such as mental substance, moral support, or something of even more value.

The people to whom I give my time, the people I consider part of in my "inner circle," and the energies that I attract all should benefit me, and vice versa.

They should make me feel full in ways I might never have imagined.

Right now, with everything that I've been through in my twenty-two years of living, I can confidently say that I don't want a lasting encounter with anyone on whom I don't imprint positively, and vice versa.

Life is very simple, but we humans insist on making it complicated.

Simplicity is the "condition or quality of being easy to understand." There is beauty in this word that, unfortunately, many often overlook. It is beautiful in that it pinpoints every problem. Nothing is left up in the air, and it gives a clear understanding of everything.

But most important, it identifies all the essentials and disregards the rest.

It creeps up on us so smoothly that majority of us miss it every time it presents itself.

I tell myself daily, *Don't overthink it, sis!*

But most times I still do. Most times I still act on emotion.

It doesn't take rocket science to know that anything or anyone that isn't essential can be categorized as a distraction and irrelevant by default.

It's just that simple.

For instance, I try to remind myself of the following, even though I'm the farthest I can be from simple most times:

- If you love someone or something, don't waste time. Make sure you don't live without him or her or it.

- If you want to be fit, maintain a healthy routine and go to the gym.

- If you dislike someone, keep your distance.

- If you aren't sure about a decision, either keep your distance or sleep, meditate, and pray on it.

For me, life doesn't seem simple in a world where most people can't reciprocate the energy I give, at least not like I need them to reciprocate. I try to never forget that everything is *temporary*, so I can't get beside myself because it won't last long.

I also feel that emotions are just another part of life. It can be complicated to learn to maneuver through them (so maybe life isn't so simple after all). To me, it's all an experience.

I do believe there is a time and place for everything in some situations, but in others, I think you just have to shoot your shot, and go with it. There won't always be a "right time."

If you need to make changes, make them accordingly.

No one has the same body chemistry as mine, nor do they have life experiences identical to mine. There are approximately seven billion people on this earth—and counting—so I'm owning *me*. You could be a twin in the same place at the same time, going through the same motions, and still have two very different interpretations of what life offered in those moments.

I'm owning my time and space on this earth in the most loving and humble way possible.

What are you doing?

Always remember: someone always needs what another person possesses.

Whether it as simple as a smile, love, kind words, encouragement, or even your presence, it is needed.

You are needed.

I am needed.

Everything changes when you emit your own frequency, rather than absorbing the frequencies around you; when you imprint your intent on the universe, rather than receiving an imprint from existence.

CHAPTER 5

All or Nothing

But if you don't love

my EVERY flaw,

then you mustn't love me—

not at ALL.

—Lang Leav

I fell in love with the above poem after reading the book *All or Nothing*. I read it over and over until the last few lines resonated with my soul, and I knew I had to share my thoughts.

Lately, I've been contemplating a variety of things that I'm not quite sure how to handle. Yet when I read this poem, a newfound understanding came over me.

These words put a lot into perspective. When I look back over my life, many situations that I have been through have led me to make an all-or-nothing decision.

Whether my goal was to get a certain reaction from someone, to reach a certain level in life, or even to decide what to wear for an event, they all had a common denominator: all or nothing. No matter what decision I had to make, I made it all the way or no way; there's no in between.

I also realized that not only did I have to choose an option but I also had to stick to it or things could get sticky fast.

I've always been told, "If you know what you want, then continuously go for it and work toward it until you get it."

All or nothing, right?

However, it's only when I'm not sure of what I want that I'm okay with settling for a happy medium. A happy medium is not always a bad thing, and sometimes temporarily living in that uncertainty works well. The best answer is not always meant to be made with extreme measures or immediately.

I've learned that taking time to be confused, thinking things through, and weighing my options can be the perfect place to be on occasion.

There is a time and place for everything.

Remember, though, that this complacency is temporary.

I can't get comfortable. The duration of this state of confusion depends on the situation and circumstance.

No matter how indecisive I was at the moment, I can't remain with a happy medium forever. It will only leave me standing for nothing and falling for anything (which was never an option).

If you've had a lot on your mind, this chapter is for you. If you've had a heavy heart lately, this chapter is for you. And if you've been indecisive, this chapter is for you.

The beginning of 2016 was not easy for me. Even though I was prepared for bumps on the road, I didn't think they would alter plans on which

I'd set my heart—but they did. Just when I thought I had my entire life planned out, God appeared and had his way.

Usually, even when I seem to be in a good mood, my heart is bleeding slowly. I'm human, and I fall into sad, dark, and discouraging places every so often. Nevertheless, I make it a point to never stay idle, to never be there long enough to distract me from my competition, which is *me*. I push through.

I don't enjoy being stressed (nor does anyone else), and I can be a bit of a crybaby at times, but I deal with stress on a frequent basis.

I'm a particular person, especially when it comes to my future, who I want around me, and what or who I let influence me. For the most part, I know exactly what I want, who I want to be, and how I want things to go, moving forward. My stumbling across hardships is inevitable because *the strongest get shaken the hardest.*

I tend to be a perfectionist, and I despise the feeling of being stagnant or lost, especially regarding the right path on my journey. I need the reality of my future to coincide with my dreams. Even so, I need to stop and reflect (that's necessary at least five times a day for me), and I have realized that I don't need to be engaged in something every second. Things still are falling together for me just a few days, weeks, or months ahead.

It's all about timing; you are exactly where you are supposed to be at the exact time you are supposed to be there.

My first semester of junior year at Temple University was insane. I'm convinced that school is a rigorous and tedious system that's designed for us to fail (kidding but not kidding), and that semester I beat myself up for being lazy with assignments, not being creative enough, and not pushing myself enough out of my comfort zone. It took a toll on me, mentally.

I told myself that I wasn't doing enough or pushing myself to my highest potential. It was discouraging because I couldn't see how I could be so versatile while trying to be great in every aspect of my life. The two did not correlate because as soon as I accomplished one side of my goals, the other side seemed to go up in flames—and the cycle never ended. It seemed impossible to balance and that was very frustrating.

To keep myself sane, I kept reminding myself of the great experience I was going to have in the spring of 2016 in other countries. I would be in South America for six months, continuing to evolve, and I would get a mini-break from the unwanted pressure—finally.

> Note: Having a creative entrepreneurial mindset, usually means you rarely ever have all your eggs in one basket, right? Yes, and this is a great thing until you try to hatch all those eggs simultaneously. Then things become unorganized and chaotic. This was me in college, and this messed me up. I attempted to start too many things at once. I tried focus and handle everything, instead of focusing on one idea at a time. That was because I was excited about all the connections I would make relating to an idea I had for a specific venture I wanted to embark on.

I've learned that doing more than one thing at a time can be tiring, and that's exactly why I don't work alone; there are some things that I have no control over and that I must leave for God.

Before I realized this, though, I felt like a single mother, in the sense that there wasn't much free time, and I always felt like I had something to do. I had to birth and care for all my miniature ventures alone, while still worrying about my infamous GPA.

Between trying to earn my bachelor's degree (at the time I had a double major of Entrepreneurship and Spanish); trying to write this book; trying to keep up with my blog posts; trying to market myself and network every chance I got; and starting the legwork in two other partnership businesses, I was beyond overwhelmed.

You may have single-mother–type stress, and if so, I know it's irritating and confusing and doesn't make sense, but I think that in life, certain things just won't happen for you until it's time—not a second before—so enjoy the ride.

I make the best of whatever is not going my way because things could always be worse and in due time, I will fly. Until it's time, I must see the struggles that I encounter as stepping stones and motivation, with my destination always in mind.

The storm is *always* necessary to reach the victory.

> There is beauty in tragedy. For tragedy has the power to motivate the human mind. It can turn weaknesses into strengths and become greatness. Why would you focus on the storm, when you can focus on the rainbow?
>
> —Mirtha Michelle Castro Marmol

I now know it's *all about perspective.*

To attain all I want, I have to give all of myself *to* myself, first. I have to rigorously learn, love, and celebrate me. This is the only way to know whether or not to accept or reject the worldly things that will come for me.

What better gift than to benefit from yourself at your highest potential?

When it's time to share all of me with someone, it will happen with such fluidity that there will be nothing to question. When God has ordained it the deed's done.

Remember that.

My potential that became my persona, my thoughts that became my words, my actions that became my habits, my habits that became my character, and my dream that became my actuality all were worth it in the end.

You get what you give, so why not give your absolute all?

CHAPTER 6

Know Yourself

The one thing that you have that nobody else has is you.

Your voice, your mind, your story, your vision.

—Neil Gaiman

The most detrimental and wasteful thing that we can do is not take the time to get to know ourselves. I've noticed that people (mostly younger) but also in general, tend to be more caught up with the artificial and materialistic aspects of life.

It's scary.

It's sad.

Have you ever heard people say they are going to be at a certain point in their lives by doing X, Y and Z, but they never push to get there? Or someone has great plans but never seems determined enough to carry them out? (All talk and no action.) Well, those people are *posers*.

What about people who say they want to be something in life that clearly is not for them, but they still try hard to fit in that space, even though their true identities are boxed away and given no chance to fight? This resistance of self is a cry for help, and the desire to be cool or socially accepted is the destruction of our authenticity.

Then, we can't forget about the people who are bold-faced hypocrites? You know, the people who are walking and talking contradictions of themselves? They say one thing, but then do another. They will tell you what they cannot tolerate or accept about you (or another person), but they have those same qualities themselves. They are inconsistent; they are fraudulent.

Practice what you preach, and do unto others as you would have them do unto you.

Just for the sake of conversation, let's target people between the ages of eighteen and twenty-five (or twenty-eight for guys, as they mature more slowly). At this point, you're in dire need of guidance. Why? Because the majority of your life is still up in the air, but this is simultaneously a crucial period that will, in many ways, shape the rest of your life.

You're probably stuck between the last days of being a teenager and not being grown up enough to completely fend for yourself. This is where, theoretically, you make a lot of mistakes, learn from them, and become better.

Realize that mistakes indicate that you are at least trying. It's perfectly fine to make errors if you stay aware that there is always room for improvement. Remember that everyone has a unique path. You will learn something that's connected to your purpose every hour, every minute, and every second until the day you leave this earth.

This resembles the many gifts of life. Take things for what they are, and just get better. Remember that these years are *crucial*, and balance is in order.

What would you say the rhythm of your life is?

Mine sits somewhere in between a pattern of orderly written cadence, intertwined in a web of keen awareness but also with untamed and jumbled thoughts, and spoken words.

Complicated? I know.

I've found it's imperative to strive for synchronization and harmony to avoid overdoing anything or wearing myself out.

We all need to work on certain issues to manifest the best versions of ourselves, so let's be slow to judge and quick to listen. Let's have the intent of being an open vessel that absorbs, assuming that many people don't have that kind of outlet.

It's important to note that understanding may or may not come afterward; either way, it's okay.

These days it baffles me that a lot of youth think that they are sensible and invincible. (I am guilty of this at times, but I'm learning to check myself faster as I grow and mature.) But I don't understand why some think they are unique when they are exactly the opposite. You can't be unique when you intentionally embody someone else to the T.

That's just being a mere duplication of a body that's already claimed.

I often see that those who try to be different are very much the same in the way they act, talk, dress, and think. Everyone rides the same wave and becomes so passionate within the art of pretending—pretending to not be, to not feel, to not deal with who they really are.

Stay away from *they*.

—DJ Khaled

It's rare to find truth these days, and it bothers me how everyone is so comfortable with their lies.

We're fed BS through television, music, blogs, social media—it's enough to knock a semi-stable person off his or her rocker. Some people are made to think they were born the wrong person and won't ever be accepted in this life.

Now, what kind of madness is that?

No matter how much you claim *not* to be a sheep, you are.

>Since when is it okay to not be who you are?

>Since when is it okay to not want to find yourself and embrace individuality?

>Since when is it cool to not be educated and speak like you don't have any sense?

>Since when is it okay to be defined by what others say is acceptable, as if society is perfect and advocates the well-being of our people, of all people?

This trend of striving for an artificial illusion of perfection, when nothing is natural or real, is disgusting.

It's draining. I can't keep up. I won't keep up.

Open your mind and heart, and realize that a flawless being *does not exist.*

If you don't have the right people around you, it is difficult—nearly impossible—to see anything outside of the box you're in, but it's possible. I know; that was me at one time. I remember a time when I hated me— literally everything about me.

I hated my skin color.

I hated that I was thicker than most of my friends.

I hated that I didn't look like what seemed to be more appealing to the opposite sex.

I hated a lot.

When I was going through my severe low–self-esteem stages, I always compared myself to what I thought I should look like, who I thought I should be, or how I should act in order to be validated.

When I was thirteen or fourteen, my sister and I visited family in Delaware, as we did once a year around New Year's. We were all talking in the living room, but I was lost in a daze. I tended to live in my head, trapped in my thoughts. This happened a lot, where for a split second, I'd have a slightly out-of-body experience while observing everyone and everything around me.

On this night, I zoned out and thought, *why can't I have a lighter complexion, like one of my cousins? Dark skin is so ugly and annoying. It's the color that everyone loves to point out and make fun of. There's never anything positive associated with what I am categorized as and who I am. I really wish I were everything* but *myself.*

Then I just blurted out to my cousin, "I wish I were your skin color or at least a shade lighter."

She looked at me and paused for a second. Then she said, "Why? I wish I had *your* skin color. It's so chocolate and so smooth and even."

> Note: When you're busy comparing yourself to others, you fail to see the beauty and riches in your own existence. Your genetic makeup is a personal and breathtaking thing. Own it.

I didn't see what she was talking about, so I just smiled and left it alone. I started looking through a magazine that was at my feet. As I flipped through the pages, I saw pictures of models that I thought I wanted to look like, and the self-hate resurfaced.

There's a difference between having a role model you would love to resemble and wanting to look like a piece of every person you see in the limelight.

I said to my older cousin, "I don't look like these girls, but I wish I did so I could be pretty and have the attention on me sometimes."

She looked at me and said, "You can't want to look like someone who isn't real. Those girls in the magazines don't even look like that."

And she was exactly right.

I can't tell you how many times after that encounter I paid close attention to models' pictures or even girls in my school, on my cheer teams who would always get the attention and cute remarks from the most attractive guys in school. I've seen people edit and edit until they look "perfect," which was completely different from what they looked like originally.

I thought it was bad when I was growing up, but it's even worse now. I see little girls who think they are supposed to be a Kardashian the people in the "I woke up like this" hashtags, with a full face of make-up on, a very loose curl in their head like that's the standard image set for beauty everywhere and everyone.

The idea that lighter is better or that a certain size is perfect has had a detrimental negative side effect within the black community. We base our lives and relationship goals of hashtags, cute pics, produced moments, and temporary videos. We base our values off the number of "likes" and comments we accumulate under any given social media post. It's all about attention. What can I do for instant gratification, despite the consequences, despite the true harm, despite the emptiness and pain, what can I do right here and now to instantly feel good about myself. To feel comfortable with who I'm not.

Many of us don't know who we are—and too many of us don't want to know either.

Don't be so quick to be in the mix.

I am my own person, and I love it. I never want to resemble another person more than I resemble myself. The day I start to do that, you'll know I'm out of line for my time, for stitching my soul's seams together, which are quite divine.

Find yourself. Know yourself. Be yourself.

Remember that you are still learning, so stop trying to teach without listening first. Don't act as if you have nothing else to go through or experience to become wiser.

Look at yourself, reevaluate your life, and come back to reality because this is where we get stuck. This is where we could lose you. I reevaluate my life at least three times a day.

Those who follow the crowd get lost in it.

I think people forget how ginormous the world is. Just because you think that you control or are known on your street, in your own neighborhood, in your own city, does not mean that you will be anything to anyone once you step foot outside of your little comfort zone. This isn't to say that you won't be, with time and effort, but initially, you are not. Nothing is handed to you; you earn it.

Be mindful not to disregard people you think you don't need.

People can only meet you, as deeply as they've met themselves. This is the heart of clarity.

—Matt Kahn

Humble yourself. Not everyone can be a rapper. Not everyone can be a model. Not everyone can be a DJ. Not everyone can be an artist. Not everyone can be famous. (Some people are famous, however, because miserable and lost people love making idiots famous for absolutely no reason but pure ignorance, filth, and hate.) Not everyone can go hard and be tough. (You're not from the streets; please stop playing yourself, sis.)

The worst thing you can do is lie to yourself. You know the truth, and you know what you have to do, so make the right moves. Everything is *not* for everybody—and that's okay because I wasn't created to be a robot; I was created to be me, in my rarest form.

My beauty began the moment I decided to be, embrace, and unconditionally love myself to the bone, through my core.

As hard as it was—and although it's been a long time coming—I am joyful that I've reached the point of love where everything that is me is starting to genuinely feed my soul.

I do that for me; no one else does that. It's all me.

Not being who you are destined to be is a waste of who God has created you to be. You may have heard that before, so live like it.

How cool is it that the same God who created mountains, oceans, and galaxies looked at you and thought the world needed one of you too?

> And the day came when the risk to remain tight in a bud
> was more painful than the risk it took to blossom.

—Anaïs Nin

You cannot get to know *you* if you are busy knowing everyone else.

Stop it.

Just stop it.

Stop all the antics, posing, and pretending. It gets old, and eventually, you'll fade out.

I hope and pray that it is not too late for you to reconnect with your absolute self. Our time here is limited, and it'd be a shame to have wasted it in pursuit of anything but yourself.

For me, it all comes down to this question:

> Who am I going to be when it's all over?

No one is you, and *that* is your power.

CHAPTER 7

Take Control

Always remember, my flower child: First they laugh, and then they copy.

The reason for my persistence in writing a book by reflecting on various aspects of my life is that I want to inspire an entire generation that has chosen not to feel—an entire generation that is lacking in patience, awareness, control, and respect.

My goal might seem silly, crazy, or impossible, but luckily for me, the bright one, I know that nothing's impossible. In fact, the word itself clearly says "I'm" possible.

Another reason is that I envision my writing turning into something great, beyond measure, so I won't stop. I won't stop because someone who doesn't know me is rooting for me, although someone who does know me is not. Sad but true.

I am in control of how I react to what the universe throws at me with regard to making my mark in life. I am responsible for how I present myself to those I intend to influence—and so are you.

For me, it's incentive enough to know that today, I am not where I want to be in life, so I must keep progressing toward the person I want to be. Remember: I am only trying to be better than the person I was yesterday. Nothing else matters.

I look past all the negative comments from insecure, attention-seeking, miserable, ignorant, and one-track-mind people. It's the only way to stay level-headed in this chaotic game called life.

When someone laughs in your face when you tell him or her your vision, as if you told a hilarious joke, it's painful and embarrassing. Yet how you take it depends on your relationship with humility.

Not every diss equates to your being unfit; rather, it solidifies that in small and narrow minds, expansion does not fit. Remember that not everyone you think should be in your corner is actually in your corner.

Once I realized why certain people were laughing and why they viewed things on such a small scale, then I got it. To them, my goals, aspirations, and dreams weren't even thought of, but they forgot I'd already cleared it with the man up above.

Anyone who's had an ounce of doubt about me as a person or about my capabilities in life will surely have a seat by the table.

To do what you do best, watch.

No one knows the places that God is taking me (including me, sometimes). God said he will bless me and will do so in front of naysayers. So thank you, Father, in advance.

I love how he works! Don't you?

Learn how valuable your mind is, so that you can never be taken for granted.

I now know it's disrespectful to my energy and peace of mind to entertain stagnancy or ignorance. I used to battle with those who were stuck in their ways. They didn't want to know any better but would knock me for what I was doing or how I was moving. They were human parasites.

But not anymore because I'm learning the importance of time and how to gracefully be free of those who don't respect my mind. I am truly one of a kind, and this is nothing but undying, bulletproof confidence.

You have to let people do what they do.

—Tayler Cloud

Yes, let people do what they do … without letting that take anything from you.

It's true that you need to be at a certain level of intelligence, open-mindedness, and awareness to relate. You need that same level with my writing so you can understand me.

- I'm aware that my vulnerability and blunt remarks aren't meant for everyone.

- I also see that my sensitivity isn't either.

- I know that my strong personality and intense emotions will not be reciprocated by everyone.

That doesn't mean I'm not valid. That doesn't mean I shouldn't have done or said something. I'm content with all of this because I control what I let affect me. I control the intensity I choose to give off. The key lies in my knowledge of the power that control has and in my using it.

At one time, I grew weary of people texting me, out of the blue, to check up on me. It wasn't that I didn't appreciate the gesture, but was it genuine? Half the time I felt like it wasn't.

I got weird and shallow vibes from most people, and it never helped that people would stop replying in text mid-conversation. They'd ask random questions that I answered, and then they'd send zero responses. I was completely over it.

My default response became, "No, don't text me to check on me. I'm alive and well, by the grace of God, and that's all you need to know."

I had to cut the leeches off. I had to carve out the mildew. Anyone who refused to grow had to go.

People aren't worried about how you're doing; they're worried about how you're doing compared to them. Discover why you're important, and then refuse to settle for any individuals who do not completely agree.

Don't do anything halfheartedly. Give it your all.

For me, one decision could be the difference between my being successful and being stagnant. That's enough for me to want to be in control of myself and anything that affects me.

This cause-and-effect is simple:

- If you are not in control of you, then you are out of control.

- If you are out of control, then you are confused.

- If you are a confused, then you are not focused.

- If you are not focused, then you don't have a plan.

- If you have no plan, there is no way to reach your goals.

- No goals equals no destination—you're stagnant.

Of course, there are many steps in between these points; these are the basics. It's also wise to never underestimate how quickly this process can fall into play. In other words, take control ASAP.

I can't stress enough that having total control over my thoughts, my responses, my actions, my reactions, and my energy is the main factor in the acceleration of my journey.

This is also the key in overcoming a lot of bullshit. I know it's tough sometimes to determine what can be controlled independently and what can't, but it's all a learning process.

When you have control over your thoughts, you have control over your life.

Read that line again.

It's okay, for example, to make the wrong decision because you think you can handle it all, but just know, you can't. Things will start to fall apart, but that's just life. (It happens to the best of us.)

Don't be like me. Don't beat yourself up about it, baby. Learning from my mistakes to build myself back up was the most challenging but rewarding decision I ever made.

A flower doesn't think of competing with the one next to it; it just simply blooms.

Being the deeply emotional being that I am, this process has been difficult for me, but it has taken a variety of opportunities and situations for me to exercise this technique with full force. I just take it one day at a time; I'm killing people with kindness and distance.

I reward love with loyalty and discomfort and doubt with distance. It's never complicated.

Start where you are. Use what you have. Do what you can.

Meanwhile, those who are secretly plotting your downfall, who can't seem to mind their own business, are playing themselves.

Those with the smallest minds often come with the biggest mouths.

Which brings us here. Pay attention, please …

I used to have a friend, someone I thought would be my friend forever. She and I were really tight from freshman year of high school to about senior year, and I called it quits around the beginning of my sophomore year at Temple.

We had the same astrological sign—Cancer—and we connected on many levels and in a lot of ways. I looked up to her. I confided in her, as she did in me. Things were as fine as they could have been for such an immature time in my life. We had some risky adventures with one another and experiences I probably would've never done with anyone if I hadn't met her when I did. During high school, for a while, things were peachy, but then I periodically noticed that some of her insecurities and toxic ways of overthinking were rubbing off on me, adding to my already insecure feelings.

I don't think that she was or is a bad person. I wish her no harm; I wish many blessings and an overflow of love and clarity because everyone is on their own journey. Sometimes, two journeys can't effectively coexist.

I still have love for that little girl, but she dug her own hole deeper and deeper within our "friendship," time after time. In addition to her personality rubbing off on me, I began to feel like everything became about her, and nothing ever translated into a positive or genuine act. I felt like she always had a motive, whether big or small.

For example, we were talking on the phone, and she asked me, "Have you and so-and-so done this?" When she couldn't tell me why she'd asked, I had to question her intentions. It was like she was fishing for information. Why would she do that? I have no idea.

At one point, my name was attached to things and situations that had nothing to do with me, and the common denominator in every instance was her and what she had said or done. I started to detect a pattern, so I continued to observe and slowly distance myself from her.

This may seem very petty, but I'm going to connect the dots soon.

The first couple of years in high school, I was figuring out who I wanted to surround myself with and who I wanted to be. Freshman year, she and I were close. She was best friends with a certain guy; I talked to him a lot during my first year at Bowie High School, but they were best friends.

(Note: I have never been a big fan of male/female friendships (although I now some can be strictly platonic), especially when both individuals are attractive, and the following scenario will support why I feel that way.)

Back then, I didn't speak up because I didn't want to cause conflict, but she would tell me questionable things about him and their friendship, and I wondered if there was something deeper between them. I wasn't suspicious at first because I knew he was very friendly, flirty, and sweet. I felt secure that he wouldn't ever cross that line with his alleged "best friend."

By junior year, a lot had happened, and I decided not to talk to him anymore, so I abruptly cut him off. We didn't speak, but we were still cordial; there was no bad blood, and I still cared about him.

By this time, he and my friend had fallen apart (to this day I don't know why), and after that, she never failed to throw dirt on his name. I never asked what had happened between them because by this time, I was almost completely mentally checked out from our friendship. I felt, though, that because of her jealousy of his actual girlfriend that something negative was bound to happen.

She was a very insecure person—I'm not condemning that because I'm insecure (less now than I was then), and we all have insecurities. But I'm not blaming my insecurities on anyone. I accept that my low self-esteem brought me to a low and questionable place, but just as you are what you eat, you also are who you associate with.

> I know that certain situations or upbringings shape people to be a certain way, and maybe they can't escape from that. It's important to detect the problem and have personal acknowledgment of an issue, along with willingness to make improvements.

I soon became even more insecure about who I was, what I was capable of, and of my being entirely like never before. I would mimic what she said about herself, which was, "I'm ugly." Yet she was far from it; she was a very pretty chocolate girl.

As time went on, it became more apparent how self-conscious I'd become. Now that I'm grown, I give credit where it's due. No matter how much wrong you did to me, I'll always stay true. Yet looking back, I sympathize because I get it.

Colorism. Self-hate. The avoidance of all blackness.

It's the true black-girl struggle, and it's something I grew up thinking was normal— that most people hated to be black; most people hated to have dark skin. You either grow into that brainwashing, or you grow out of it.

From then on, one fallen door led to the next one and so on. Exhaustion continued to build up on my end, to the point where I was over our conversations always just being about her.

You may have that draining friend—someone I hope, after reading this, you'll let go as well.

Don't get me wrong; I'm a great listener. I'll listen to you vent all day because I know it's important, and I genuinely care—if you are sincere. But if every time we talk, you talk only about yourself or about the same issue that you don't really want to solve, something is wrong. If you don't want my honest opinion, or when I talk about my own life, you turn the conversation back around to you, something is wrong!

Red flag! Abort mission!

That is exactly what I was experiencing.

We would gossip about people and things that were irrelevant, and more than once, I thought, *Why is she asking me questions that have absolutely nothing to do with her? What is the motive here?*

Of course, everyone occasionally shares gossip—it's good for the soul (could be debateable)—but when you constantly need to know about other people's misfortune, downfall, or mishaps, there's an issue. I never knew her intention, but if it walks, talks, and looks like a duck, then it's more than likely a duck, sis. At least that's what I'd been taught.

She'd ask me things like, "Are you still a virgin?" How would you react to this question? Was I wrong for being hesitant in my answer?

I feel certain topics should be organically communicated and never forced upon you. Otherwise, all you'll get is an awkward facial expression because I don't want to tell you, but I care enough about our friendship or your potential reaction to my being disrespectful to not be blatantly rude. (I always wonder how people will take the things I say.)

Plus, I'm a private person, so I would question the intentions of someone who would ask me something like that so effortlessly. Why did she want to know? Yes, we would talk about things like that but it was in a setting where something of that nature was already the topic of discussion, not just randomly. If I'd answered, what would she have done with that information? The thing is, if I'd wanted her to know, then I would have told her—without her grilling me about it.

I wasn't going to be receptive to her asking me that same question every time she brought up the topic of sex.

Finally, by senior year, I had smartened up a bit. I wasn't going to tell her anything; I'd just let her think what she wanted to think. That's what you have to do with people who think they know it all, with people who think they know you better than you do.

I had cut her off but not completely. She was kind of dangling on a string with me, but she didn't know it. And in the same year, the straw that broke the camel's back occurred.

I'd reached a point of cringing each time she reached out to me, fearing that what I'd hear would upset or annoy me. I hated having the unbearable, "It's always something with you" feeling. That's a red flag!

Adding to this foolishness, she apparently spread a rumor about me, telling a friend of a friend that I was making negative comments about her. At the time, it bothered me, and I asked the friend of a friend if she knew why my ex-friend felt animosity toward me.

She said, "She told me, but I forget."

Convenient.

One day soon after, we were all in the same place, and I decided it would be a good time to address the problem. I cut to the chase and confronted the situation because I was genuinely confused. Why did she have such strong feelings against me, especially when we didn't really hang out anymore.

When I asked her, she said it was because I'd made comments about her "boy toy" and said that she was just like one of the guys, rather than her being his girl. (It was basically childish drama.)

I paused. I could have denied making such comments, but to be honest, I didn't even have the energy. That day, I told myself that might be the last straw for our "friendship" because she was putting words in my mouth while pretending to not know anything—*and* throwing me under the bus.

Moreover, I later learned something about the boy who was best friends with my ex-friend. As I mentioned, he and I talked a lot freshman year. He and I still were acquaintances, but we'd been talking a bit more frequently than usual. It was cute, calm, and as casual as it could be, but anyone who has been in love knows you can't be "friends." So it was one of those situations but nothing too extreme.

Like an idiot, I told my friend that he and I had been talking again, and of course that didn't end well because she constantly threw dirt on his name. Suddenly they weren't "best friends" anymore, and she said certain things about him in front of me every chance she got, as if she didn't know that I had strong feelings for him and, even more obviously, as if they were never best friends.

When she did this, I asked myself why she was so angry. Why was she so hurt that they'd fallen apart if they were just friends?

She told me they'd slept in the same bed but was quick to say that nothing happened. She told me about a time when they were in the mall, and she was in the dressing room, and he made a comment about her body. He gave her a foot massage and things of that nature. She also mentioned that one of her friends thought the reason they had fallen apart as best friends was because he was beginning to have romantic feelings for her.

Again, I wondered why she was telling me these things. *Is this a joke?* I wondered. *Is this my actual life? What are your true intentions? Are you jealous? Are you just trying to hurt me? Why am I just now seeing all this?*

Once again, however, I let it slide.

I made excuses for everything that had transpired between us. I was still defending her because that's just how I was, and part of me didn't want to believe that what God was blatantly showing me over and over: it was time to let go.

When you're as stubborn as I can be at times, you have to be placed in situations that almost crush your spirit before you will listen. And that's exactly what God did.

At the beginning of my sophomore year at Temple, around homecoming, God moved for the last time on this situation. My friend called me to ask who was performing at the homecoming concert because she wanted to come. I didn't want her to come, and I didn't need any extra stress. Most of the time, she just said outrageous things that make me question it all.

Regardless, she ended up coming for homecoming, arriving very late on Friday night, along with some other friends of hers. (I knew they were coming, but I didn't know them.) When they arrived, they came in to see the house and meet my roommates. We all sat and talked for a minute.

You may have heard the saying, "You're only as good as the company you keep." This definitely applied to her with her friends—no good. Loud. Irritating. Obnoxious. Ignorant. They were loud, shallow, and, as I later found out, fake as hell.

After we talked for a bit, we took them to their designated places in Philly. I was very stand-offish and irritated because I felt her presence brought negative energy. I guess I didn't try very hard to mask my feelings, but I later found out they made negative comments about me. I'm sensitive, so that did bother me.

The next morning as we were getting ready for an eventful day, not even twenty minutes into my morning, the BS began. She asked me why I always seemed mad. I didn't give too much of a response because she didn't really want to hear what I had to say anyway. Then she said that her friends had asked why I was so bitter and "a bitch."

I left that alone too. I was shocked that her friends—people I didn't know—had been talking about me with an alleged "friend" of mine. I was shocked that she had expressed their concerns in a tone that suggested she agreed with them. I was shocked that she had the audacity to relay that message to someone she called a friend, instead of defending me.

I realized that she didn't know why I was "mad, sad, bitter" all the time because she didn't care about anything but herself and her problems. I had no energy to debate with her. I was drained.

When it was almost time to go to the game, she stops to check her snapchat and said, out of the blue, "I don't understand how he can watch my snaps but not speak to me in person." We hadn't been talking about this boy; she just randomly but conveniently brought him up to see if I would spill information, but I was too smart for that. I brushed it off with, "Not my business or my concern," but my irritation was building rapidly. I held my tongue, but I didn't know how long I could do that—she was staying for the entire weekend.

After the game, when we were on the bus back to campus, she again brought up his name. I didn't offer any information, but my feelings for him were all over my face, so she asked, "How are you guys?" I assumed she asked because she knew that I had been seeing him and talking to him recently.

I said, "We are fine. We are friends, nothing serious." That was a lie, but she and I were no longer close, so I wouldn't willingly tell her anything. I wouldn't have cared if he had just broken my heart; I would not tell her *anything*. In my head I'm like, "We're good, slim. Don't trip."

I was being vague, and she always complained that I didn't tell her things, but that was because the information I'd tell her always seemed to get around. I didn't have time for people who didn't know how to keep their mouths shut about other people's business or keep their noses out of people's business.

I hesitated, but then, for some reason, I added, "He doesn't trust me." I immediately knew that I'd messed up—big time! Right after those words slipped from my mouth—because it was heavy on my heart—I had an uneasy feeling.

Either she didn't notice my body language or didn't care because she then said, "What do you mean? He doesn't trust you? Like, how?"

By this time, my guard was down, and I foolishly thought, *It's fine. I can tell her why, but I just won't go into detail. What's the worst she can say?* Maybe she'd say something supportive or encouraging, even if it wasn't what I wanted to hear, and then life would go on.

I said, "He doesn't trust me in the sense that he believes I'll do what I did before, like I'll give up on him—on us—and break his heart." I know that I'm sensitive, but I was not prepared for her response—at least not from a *friend*.

70

She effortlessly said, "Oh, yeah, that makes complete sense. You're very wishy-washy and indecisive."

I thought, *I know this. I acknowledge this, and I accept the consequences for my actions. But that doesn't mean I'm a terrible person. It means I'm human, and I mess up, as we all do, so screw you.*

To me, she basically alluded to the fact that I was a heartless soul, that I was the same immature girl from high school who didn't know what she wanted. And possibly would intentionally or not break his heart again.

Now, while it is a fact that I am indecisive. Don't you think I would've taken the necessary time to reevaluate my reasons for deciding to talk to him again. Why could I not get that credit? Why is it so hard to believe that I've self-reflected, identified my toxic traits and have taken the necessary steps to improve?

No, you just want me to stay mediocre, huh? Cool.

She inferred that although I desperately needed love, I didn't deserve it—or maybe I just didn't deserve it from him.

This caught me off guard and pushed me over the edge because I'd been expecting a different response.

Everyone else that I told about my situation—knowing me, knowing how I was, how we were, and how I felt about him—sensibly asked, "Why wouldn't he trust you?" The difference was that they defended my character instead of questioning or willingly demolishing it.

It's not that I wanted people to tell me what I wanted to hear, but she could have been more considerate and concerned as my friend. She and he didn't even speak anymore, but she stuck up for him and disregarded me entirely.

Snake.

I would hope that my friends would point out when I was wrong but not define me by my mistakes or throw things in my face. It was clear at that point that she didn't know me and that her intentions were ill driven.

Other people don't know the depth of that situation because it was five years ago, and no one was as close to him as she was. He told her absolutely everything, and she would then pick and choose information to tell me. But she'd have me think that I was the crazy one.

From a friend, I expected something like, "Have you both been working on that aspect?"—something that showed she understood that I was striving to be better in this life. She should not have blamed me and blatantly suggested that he should leave me alone because I was a messed-up individual, emotionally and mentally, and so I'd inevitably play him, when that was not the case.

She almost said it like I enjoyed hurting him. That's not who I am. I'd made a mistake, yes, but that wasn't the extent of my character.

A "friend" wouldn't and shouldn't do that.

Don't allow it.

I sure didn't.

From then on, I felt like any and all of her objectives toward me were harmful, and I couldn't deal with her anymore.

Just like that.

Mentally, I'd already cut her off.

Now, remember this occurred while we were on the bus, so as soon as we got back to my house, I left her in my room, walked outside, and called my older sister.

This bothered me so much. I was already dealing with trying to gain his trust back because he was who I really wanted to be with *at the time*. So for her to just say what she said, with no hesitation, spoke volumes and added fuel to my internal fire.

I told my sister what had happened and then I broke down into tears. While sobbing, I said, "I don't understand how people can judge me or feel like they know me so well when there is so much more inside that no one has even tapped into. No one ever seems to stick around long enough to discover me. I realize that I'm not the easiest person to deal with, but you can't be that scary for someone worth it, can you? I'm just labeled as the bitter, bitchy, lonely, selfish, and heartless person, but no one knows or cares to know the real Chántelle, and I'm truly over this."

I was broken. Shattered. Exhausted. My heart was bleeding uncontrollably when I heard the words, *"When are you going to stop pouring your sweet fragrance out for those who aren't worthy?"*

I now know that was the Holy Spirit, telling me that this journey (and others) would end much sooner than I thought.

Shortly afterward, I got myself together. I took the wonderful advice from my sister and prayed that God would get to Sunday without exploding.

I walked back in the house but didn't say one word. I was oblivious to every word she said after that moment. I went numb for the rest of that weekend. It was only Saturday, and I was so ready for her to go. And when she left, that was the last time we spoke.

That was the end.

God showed me how he works, and I heard him loud and clear.

It's true—people want to get at me. They want to make me feel uncomfortable about the moves I make, as if they're far beyond my reach. Yet they are sadly mistaken because I will continue to always be in firm control of me!

This is where I started to flourish. I do my own thing, I stay in my own lane, and I ignore the hype because I have an open mind for many things, but it's attached to nothing.

Stay in control, stay fearless, and stay focused because *they* hate to see you unbothered, let alone unstoppable.

They tried to bury me but didn't realize I was a seed.

CHAPTER 8

Solitude

To make the right choices in life, you have to get in
touch with your soul. To do this you need to experience
solitude, which most people are afraid of because in the
silence you hear the truth and know the solutions.

—Deepak Chopra

The unfortunate part about this reality is that most people on earth will
never experience the depth or the significance of true and absolute *solitude*.

In this day and age, being alone is somehow equated to being weak, weird,
"less than," lonely, and/or miserable. For some reason, many are ashamed
to reside in solitude, to be in tune with what's inside.

For instance, would you ever consider going alone to a social event,
assuming you're familiar with the people and/or surroundings? Most of
you more than likely would not. But why not?

I understand that people like being accompanied in the world we live in
now, for safety reasons, but I think a lot of the concern is in our heads.
You don't need a "squad" for every single place you go to?

Ask yourself why you're so resistant to being alone. From what are you
hiding?

What don't you want people to realize about you?

What don't you want to admit to yourself about yourself?

How long are you going to put up a front?

As I was preparing to write this chapter, I realized that I've lived in solitude for the past eight years, but I still hadn't spoken on it in depth. I think that being reluctant to be alone has more to do with internal factors than external ones.

The current generation, in general, is socially awkward; everything is done for show. People may think they should go to a certain place with this person or that person because everyone is going to be there, and they don't want anyone to think they don't have friends; they don't want to look dumb or weak.

I think that's pathetic.

Go by yourself. Market yourself. Show your confidence and your security. In the end, you'll get all the attention you're looking for, and people will be attracted to you for all the right reasons.

Next question: do you like to sit in a space and just think about life? No phone. No Wi-Fi. No pen or pencil. No computers. No games. Just you, your thoughts, and God.

I do this all the time. I take myself away because I am always tuned into what's happening, and it wears on my mental, emotional, and spiritual being. Because of social media, we're often expected to be "in the know." We rarely stop to take it all in.

Inhale.

Exhale.

Just be.

Realize deeply that the present moment is all you ever have.

—Eckhart Tolle

In general, most people are afraid of being alone. As for me, I'd much rather go anywhere alone than to be with people all the time, especially those whose character or energy I don't care for. I frequently say, "I don't like people." I usually say it with a smile or a little chuckle, but I am dead serious. People get on my nerves and can be annoying.

I'm not antisocial, but I do appreciate my "me" time. And I'm learning not to feel bad for making time for myself because giving people too much of me has consistently contributed to my downfall and hindered my elevation. It's suffocating.

I love and respect myself too much to engage in activities or interact with people who threaten my peace of mind. I just like to be left alone sometimes, and I don't think that's bad. I like to be in my own space, in my own thoughts, and in my element, just vibin', because this is where I begin to manifest. My need for solitude might have to do with my moody personality initially, but regardless serves a greater purpose. Everyone needs some solo time periodically.

I'm not encouraging you to fall off the face of the earth or isolate yourself from life; that's not healthy. Just be selective and be observant of those around you.

Think about it: how can you be serious about you if you are never solely with just you? The answer—and I want to make this very clear—is that you can't. Those who say they're serious about themselves and their endeavors but never are alone are kidding themselves. It's that simple.

Get your mind right, and stop playing yourself because we see you.

I want you to find bliss in companionship, to find a home in another being whom God has prepared for you. But first, I want you to reach all that your heart desires in you. Discover genuine comfort and wholeness in you. Create a safe haven and nurture it daily—for you—first.

If you don't, seeking those things in another, will never work. Being in solitude for a time is the root of everlasting tranquility. Find it. You can be alone and still be happy. You can be alone and not be lonely.

A lot of people have told me, "You're lonely. That's why you're bitter."

But I'm *not* lonely, and I'm very loved. When I'm alone, it is by choice.

Being alone and content is not the same as being lonely and depressed. Now more than ever, I know the importance of working on myself and of perfecting me, my craft, my joys, and my pleasures of my heart.

I do admit, though, that making me the greatest I can be before sharing myself, my space, and my life with another is tough. I'm not sure why, but I tend to push love and warmth away the second I feel it, yet it's the very thing I'd give my life to have.

I don't understand my own logic; I have no idea why I do it, but I know that God has not forgotten about me. His timing is perfect, and that is all I need.

Some people struggle with solitude, doing their best to avoid it, and they shame others who enjoy it. Some will never know themselves. They will never know what it's like to face themselves. They condemn and run away from everything that reflects them and their natures, every chance they get. Don't blame others if you're constantly defined by someone's idea of you, based on their ideologies and beliefs. That's no one's fault but your own.

Of course, it's possible to have lonely moments when in solitude.

It is not easy.

It is not easy.

It is not easy.

It is not easy.

But nothing worthwhile ever is easy, my darling.

The truth is that I still have days when I question everything about me and why I am here. But then, I just figure, *Well, would I really be if the world didn't need me?*

No, I wouldn't. It's clear that the universe is very particular and that God is intentional. With that dynamic combination, how could I ever have any doubt? I couldn't. I am here for a reason, not for a season, and so are you.

Basking in solitude and walking in it confidently sets the ultimate tone for strength. It prepares you for knowing how to get through hell without being dependent on anyone. Although I get criticized for boasting about my solitude, I still thrive.

I still go on.

I still learn.

I still pray.

And my life still carries on faithfully.

People often fail to realize the connectivity of it all. I choose to be alone because I feel it's a waste of time to try to get others to see me and my perspective and to feel me when they weren't meant to do so. Things like that must come organically or not at all.

It's a choice, and I choose me. This concept is something that half-grown, shadowed minds will never grasp. I am *mature* enough to admit that I have lonely moments, some days more than others. Some days are darker than others, but I also know that I'm never truly alone. Thank you, heavenly Father; you always bring me back.

Some say, "She's alone now, but she won't be alone for long." You can bet on that. For those of you who have a fear of yourself, don't worry about my journey of getting to know myself.

> Queen, big changes are coming. Even though the process may be
> painful, rest assured that the end shall speak. Whatever you feel
> you are losing will be restored. ... You are being realigned and
> recalibrated because it's time to fulfill your soul's purpose. Don't
> get side tracked nor distracted. This is what awakening feels like.

—"The Queen Code"

Some have said that in the end, all you have is yourself. I agree. Solitude is bliss.

> Without great solitude, no serious work is possible.

—Picasso

Many people are confused by or stressing over someone other than themselves. I am here to tell you to *stop*. Stop wasting your precious time because you don't get it back. He or she isn't worth it—not at all.

As hard as it might be, stop worrying about the wrong things. Let it go, and trust the process. If you are meant to be with someone, you will be. Let it go, and pray that everything comes full circle. If anything you shared with another mind, body, and soul was genuine, then it will come back.

Be at peace with knowing you gave your all, knowing you're still a work in progress, and knowing that you genuinely tried the best you could for something or someone you believed in.

> Plant your garden and decorate your own soul, instead
> of waiting for someone to bring you flowers.

—Jorge Luis Borges

Live your life.

Travel the world.

Fall in and out of love.

Make mistakes, and learn as much as you can.

Don't sweat the small stuff.

Give out the energy you want to receive.

I'm learning to appreciate loss. Anything that's meant to journey with me can't leave me, no matter how hard it tries. Forcing relationships equates to being stagnant, and I can't do that. Moving backward never is an option.

The only thing I can do is move forward, and I hope I see you there.

CHAPTER 9

Chaos

It's a boundless and daring feeling to be secure, to know that you are honest and true with each move you make, so much so that nothing outside of that element can ever dismantle who you are.

Untouchable, unbothered, and poised at its finest defines me, right now.

If you real, you'd recognize.

—August Alsina

When you have been humbled, when you have worked tirelessly to do right by others but repeatedly have dealt with people's disrespect, you owe it to yourself to do the following:

- Thank God that you made it without any bloodshed.

- Acknowledge and celebrate your progress.

- Take pride in yourself.

- Reward yourself.

Yes, reward yourself for not losing your mind when you probably should have a long time ago. Have the audacity to celebrate you. (If you don't, who will?)

Practice reckless faith with shameless audacity. It's not about how hard you get hit but how hard you get hit and still have the power move forward.

It's amazing to me that one day a person can be on the verge of losing it all and then, the next day, still be here to reflect on that.

The chaos didn't kill me—it hasn't killed me—but it has tried. Not everyone can say they overturned that which was sent for their destruction and that led to the continued development of their minds and mentalities.

Yet I can.

The mind is such a powerful source that when you discover how to discipline it, your failures become buoyant because you'll always recover. With that, you can never be defeated.

Stay mindful of that. Don't be too hard on yourself.

> If everything is dipped in gold, then baby, it will never
> grow. Everything sweet ain't sugar-coated.

—Jhene Aiko

I can embrace and adapt to change. I am emotionally intelligent.

Claim it.

You don't have to look a certain way or be born into a certain status to know and flaunt your worth. Your progression is just as valid as those for whom it seemingly comes natural. Recognize that! Stop belittling yourself. Stop comparing your work to others looking for reasons why one is more or less superior than the other. That's chaotic insanity.

That's also one of my bad habits.

As I've mentioned, I attended Temple University, majoring in entrepreneurship and minoring in Spanish. I received my BBA (bachelor of business administration) in February 2018.

Throughout my college years and even before I accepted Temple as my second home, I knew that I would study abroad. That was a must; studying Spanish was a must; and being my own boss was a must!

I had to choose avenues that would suit me in the long run, and, thankfully, those all fit. I went through hell and high water to get there, but I finally studied abroad in spring 2016—and I fought for that.

I was told many times that I couldn't study abroad. I was given the run-around. I was advised numerous times to hold off until after I graduated to study abroad. But I stuck with it. I told myself, "Yes, you can!"

I had made up my mind that I was going abroad, and I was going while I was in school. I didn't see the value in waiting to have this unforgettable experience, so I didn't give up.

The course was a whirlwind study, but it was worth it when I touched the soil of five different countries within six months. From January to July, I was out and about in South America, just being great. I was in Ecuador, Uruguay, Argentina, Chile, and Brazil, and the experience was marvelous!

South America wasn't ready for me, but I wouldn't trade any of it for the world.

As I've mentioned, I don't just have a dream; I also have a plan for everything I have my mind and heart set on in this life. Having a clear-cut and passionate intent on something is key, and it helps gauge tough decisions when you're on your way.

Remember that a goal without a plan is just a dream.

There are too many magnificent dreams floating around in this world that never reach fruition. Why is that? Is it that people don't have the tools, or are they just too lazy to apply themselves? Maybe it's not that black or white; there usually are a lot of gray areas with everything.

One thing is evident, however, and that is, for some odd reason, the youth today think they're owed something. In actuality, they owe it to the world to make something of themselves, to relieve the motherland of the chaos that was embedded in past times.

It's a reality that nothing that can be altered without education, persistence, and unity.

Traveling and exploring other countries and cultures opens you up and allows you to be more cognizant of the ways of the world. My opinions, including those that follow, reflect that worldview. Here it goes:

I don't appreciate that the US Congress makes all the laws for us colored folks but couldn't care less if we see the light of day going forward. I also don't appreciate that Congress refused to cooperate with President Barack Obama (disappointing but not surprising), mainly because he was black.

Wherever you stand on politics, I think all decisions should take into consideration that everyone on earth has value. As humans, we do not have the authority, regardless of any laws, written or unwritten, to assign worth to another individual. Even though this was done in slavery, it's simply inhumane and unjustifiable.

It is brutal that the United States trained armies in countries around the world to use during dictatorships (whose placement we were responsible for). This is only half of what white America has encouraged regarding inhumane activities around the world, but I can only stomach discussing so much. You can do the research.

I know right-wing conservatives probably won't agree with me, and that's cool. Just be aware that if they find loopholes, raping and humiliating an entire race of people ("minorities") silently, they will have to answer for their actions publicly.

And this has already come to fruition, with Pence and his puppet playboy Donnie, currently in office. I still don't know how that happened. Allowing heinous acts to occur and killing off people as you please will backfire soon. Personally, I am on no extreme of the political spectrum. I believe in balance. Taking care of people while making more than enough money surpasses sustainability. People are just filthy and greedy.

Moral: stop being greedy.

White America has been the biggest of bullies for decades and minding the business of other countries for decades. We are a broken country. We need to practice self-help. We have our own crisis here to fix first regarding race, regarding a nation that was built on the backs of slaves and fueled by discrimination and hate. It's time for the tables to turn.

It's long overdue, and no matter who you are, you know it too. That truth either scares you or excites you. It's pure and utter chaos. It's imperative to be educated. If you don't like the system, then be the system.

I'm all for business, but I'm also for taking care of the only race that matters—the human race. We are indirectly all connected. It doesn't matter how much you worked to build America or how many acres of land were passed down to you from previous generations. At the end of the day, we are all just renting this space.

Don't try to dictate the way people should live or who should live and who shouldn't, as if you gave them life. It's awful.

Again, education is key. Whether you go to school or not, educate yourself. Make sure you know who you are, and stay confident in what you know so that injustice, selfishness, and greed can finally cease.

I could say a lot more, but I won't. Just let that sink in, and realize that we are all one people, and the people are the power.

Moving on, I look around my campus all the time and see people going through the motions. Often, I sit back and say to myself, "The majority of you don't want what I want from life. You know nothing about putting in that work. You aren't willing to starve to make your mark in life, and you definitely don't want it as bad as I do."

That might sound a bit cocky, but it's true, so yes, I will toot my own horn. If you have the same mind-set, you won't take offense. I honestly wonder what people are thinking when they are twenty-five–plus years old and already graduated from college but are doing nothing with their degrees. They wasted time and money to obtain it, and have the nerve to ask, "Where are the parties?"

No, the question is, "Where are your priorities?" I am dying to know. Why do you snap and/or post your every move? No one cares that much; I promise. Come on, now. Everyone knows when you're really moving—it's done in silence—so say less. Seriously, go find some business, and be on your merry way.

Some people will want to be around you just because they see your treasure and your drive to become greater, so they stick around so they can use you. In other words, people are just trying to "come up" off the next person's "come-up."

That's weak. You can do better. No one wants success for the next person, let alone themselves, nowadays. The disguised envy is mind-blowing.

Be aware:

- The mixy behavior must stop.

- The girls/guys you're always around will get old at some point.

- You can't keep doing the same lame/fake things with the same lame people and expect different results.

- You can't keep posing and playing games for no reason because time will expose the real you.

The chaos must end eventually. Do you want to be fruitful and elevate? I'm sure you do. Hold yourself accountable. You can do it!

My father used to say, "There is a time and a place for everything."

Know when your time is up for certain people, events, and situations. If you don't know, time will gladly do the honors by rudely reminding you.

Thank me later, thanks for nothin', thanks for bluffin'
thank you so, so much for wearin' your true colors.

—Drake

Showing me who you were made my life a lot easier. I can't respect it. I can smell leeches from a mile away. Never try me. You only cross me once.

The thing about chaos is that while it disturbs us, it too forces
our hearts to roar in a way we secretly find magnificent.

—Christopher Poindexter

How does chaos have you moving?

CHAPTER 10

Shades

The truth is rarely pure and never simple.

—Oscar Wilde

When people show you who they really are, believe them the first time.

—Maya Angelou

When you're hurting, is the truth really the best medicine?

I honestly don't know. It could depend on the circumstances.

People may debate that the truth could lead to more unnecessary pain. I can see that, but I can also see things from the other end of the spectrum. I wouldn't lie to anyone to save their feelings, if the truth was in their best interests.

If someone lied to me, I'd want to know the truth, even if it hurt me. But that's just me. Some people would rather sacrifice that truth for false delight.

Most of us seem to pretend to be happy about how we're doing each day, not just externally but internally. Everyone owns a pair of shades that projects the picture that they are always okay.

For instance, you run into someone who asks, "How are you doing?"

Most likely, your default reply is, "I'm good. How are you?"

The words "I'm good" probably roll off your tongue. It's an automatic reaction instead of a thoughtful reply.

So why do we even bother to ask how someone is doing when we don't care about a response (not to mention that the response probably isn't true)?

I hate that shallow behavior is now socially accepted as the norm. Many people are passive/aggressive, and this also has been normalized. That bothers me. It concerns me.

A common little white lie that I tell someone daily is "I'm okay," or "I'm good. Don't worry about me." Those are my programmed responses—the things I say in response to empty concern from insincere people, which seems like almost everyone.

We're going through the motions. We're shying away from real issues that affect us. We're failing to address pain because we equate feelings with weakness. It's backwards, yet it's so common.

This is something I frequently ponder: If it's no one's business how I feel, why does it feel good when someone makes it their business, without associating me with misfortune, regardless of how I appear?

Because I'm supposed to because although sometimes it's overwhelming, I crave to feel.

In the same breath, I don't want to be anyone's headache. Who does? It's something I struggle with severely. I never want anyone to feel they should carry my pain, worry, concerns, doubt, or trials along with theirs. Everyone carries something, whether they acknowledge it or not.

I'm independent, but emotional and sensitive; feisty but delicate; annoying but lovable; and the motherliest yet tender person you'll ever come to know.

The furthest thing from perfect, like everyone I know.

—Drake

I can appreciate when people have the confidence and wisdom to show they aren't invincible, especially if they are celebrities. Sharing your flaws and self-doubt, particularly as an artist, brings purpose to your platform.

A couple of years back, when Bryson Tiller began to merge with mainstream music, he seemed so mysterious to me. I liked it; I liked him. He reminded me a lot of myself, for some reason, so I did some research on him—listened to some interviews and searched on Google. I found out a lot of details about his character and personality from things that he said and didn't say.

I thought, *Wow. He's as genuine as his music. He seems to be a true individual who doesn't want to disconnect from being who he is, regardless of fame.*

I admire people who are not afraid to be who they are and who recognize and accept their influence. I listened to one of his interviews in which he mentioned why he prefers audio interviews to video interviews and why he will probably never record his interviews.

"It's weird seeing myself," he said.

Even though he said little, I read a lot, and it was clear he was humble and focused, despite everything we saw as glamorous. He wasn't changing for anyone. That's dope, and I love it.

As I continued to listen, his words again hit home for me and inspired me to write this section of my memoir. He spoke about his earlier years in Kentucky and noted that his status of becoming a full-time known artist never had been on his radar because he wasn't noticed, ever.

"In high school, I didn't have that many friends and nobody cool really liked or spoke to me."

That broke my heart, but it also resonated with me. I thought, *Would I have been that person who talked to him in high school?* Then I was honest with myself: *More than likely, nope. I wouldn't have been.*

It bothered me to come to that realization because now I would be that person who would want to be his friend and be so low-key. It made me think of what I dealt with in terms of status in high school.

Flashback: I was on the cheerleading squad, but what did that really mean? People might've thought that I was "popular," but the truth is, no matter how many events I attended or how many "known" people I was around, I never felt like I was one of them as much as it seemed like I was. Overall, I felt like I just didn't belong.

Out of all my cheer-mates, regular friends, and even cousins, I was, most of the time, never the girl who guys gave their attention to. I was always called "cute," like a bunny rabbit or something, instead of "sexy" or "bad."

I was rarely anyone's type—ever.

I was too dark, or too manly, as far as my figure. Broad shoulders, long arms, and big hands wasn't the standard of attraction for anyone. Although I don't think I had all those unappealing features on my body, I timidly and secretly began to believe that it was true. For most kids, I just wasn't "it."

I don't know what it was, but the guys I had crushes on overlooked me, time and time again, for one of my friends. This really hammered at any self-esteem I had begun to rebuild, as the silent rejection occurred continuously. I was going for the shallow people with basic qualities. I always ended up disappointing myself because, little did I know, I was not a shallow person and never could be.

I wasn't built to fit in. I am custom-made, baby.

However, I'm human, and my insecurities ate at me. I compared myself to others, and I became jealous of the attention others got, of that "thing"

I just didn't seem to embody for these male beings, by whom I wanted to be accepted so badly.

I battled demons—jealousy and envy and none other than my friends. I was always comparing myself to them, focusing on what I lacked. It was a hectic time, and I've never said that until this book. I'm so happy they were who they were and that I grew how I grew. I would've regretted it till this day if I had made a reckless decision that jeopardized any of my friendships due to my insecurities.

In Bryson Tiller's interview, he shared that no one liked him, and that triggered a feeling in me that I'd kept buried for a long time. It sparked the sadness I'd felt when no one wanted me. It reminded me that I was never anyone's first choice but rather an afterthought. With my sensitivity, little things like that would get to me. Over time, I made mental notes that I never spoke aloud but held on.

I don't know if it was because of my skin color, or that I was never as fit as I wanted to be, or that I never had the image with the long, mixed hair or tracks, but it messed with my head and how I saw myself.

This brings me to an even bigger and more prevalent issue I dealt with—colorism, when it came to *shades*. I mirrored people who were socially accepted, in hopes of receiving that outside validation myself. Young black girls, particularly those who are darker skinned, get shut down, especially by the young black males, the harshest and too often. As if black isn't just black.

The most disrespected person in America is the black woman.

The most unprotected person in America is the black woman.

The most neglected person in America is the black woman.

—Malcolm X

Colorism labels and detaches you from you. It nitpicks and separates the "prettier" and acceptable shades of black from the "uglier" and less acceptable shades of it. This concept is one of the most demeaning discriminatory standards, and I was introduced to it in elementary school.

Kids are mean. Kids learn behavior. Racism and colorism are learned behaviors.

We never heard it, but we knew we had to be the "right" shade of black to be accepted or treated with favor. In the case of guys showing interest in me, nine times out of ten they wouldn't look twice at me because of my complexion. I was existing without being noticed. If I ever *was* noticed, it was because I had something to say, and that was always equated to my being negative. Suddenly, I was doing too much; I was seen as angry, bitter. I hate people. (Did I mention that already?) I really do.

High school was high school, and now I'm seeking something new. In hindsight, I get why they weren't looking my way, and it had nothing to do with me.

God said, "I want more for you. Just be patient while I bypass all this crap for you."

I'm still waiting. I'm not complaining, but it can be a lonely and scary process at times. To be honest, I'm scared to be in love with someone who never falls in love with me, who just pretends to, or who can't ever love me as thoroughly as I need him to. I'm scared that I've been alone for so long that I won't know how to be with someone if the time ever does come. I'm afraid I'll crawl back into my shell and end up pushing my soul mate completely away. I'm so used to being independent, picking up my head, and comforting myself that I don't know if I'll ever be open to receiving that from someone else.

Some days I don't feel like trying or reaching out to anyone, but I still go through shit. That's the death of me. Most days I'm on the verge of tears. I have tears for different reasons, of course, but they are still tears. Worry, uncertainty, and fear of how things will turn out for me. I recently told my best friend that I'm not sure if I know how to be genuinely happy anymore. That scares me.

It seems that every time I get close to something or someone I perceive to be real and genuine, the outcome fails me. I can only be disappointed about one time per person or situation before I'm over it. I have a very low tolerance for foolishness and deceit.

People seem to be okay with the idea of being happy and satisfied. I often see those people living in a haze of bullshit. Everyone walks around with their shades on (literally and figuratively). The shades block them from reality and keep them bottled up in their own utopias, where everything is great, and the actions they make don't have consequences.

Then there are the people who claim to always be joking and playing. That's BS. I'm fed up with people putting on fronts. I'm sick and tired of people trying to mask true feelings to lighten a mood. I see right through you, so get your life together and stop using jokes as a cover-up. I know you weren't joking. You know you were serious. So just own it. It's shady. It's childish. It's scary. Your aura reeks.

The truth is told in jokes.

—Romanian proverb

I'm not saying this to ostracize anyone because we've all been shady or hidden from ourselves at some point, even me. I am guilty. I can be petty. I have no problem admitting when I'm wrong and highlighting that I am flawed all over.

I've been oblivious to how my actions and choices affected others or the consequences they'd bring. Yet when I realized that no good came from my shying away from the truth because it was always there, I corrected my faults—or tried to, at least.

The truth is like the sun. You can shut it out
for a time but it ain't goin' away.

—Elvis Presley

> Three things that cannot be hidden for long:
> the sun, the moon, and the truth.
>
> —Buddha

That's how serious the force of truth is. Don't be like the masses and foolishly dismiss it. At the end of the day, there is no logic in pretending to be happy, in pretending to be cool, in pretending to be unbothered. Feel it. The truth will set you free.

If you need help, ask for it.

If you need to talk to someone, reach out.

If you feel a certain way, then voice it.

Why have you put it off for so long? What are you waiting for? What is holding you back?

It's frightening to let anything have that much control over you, so much that you're constantly running away from your mind, from yourself, from opportunities and time. The *shades* don't love you like you love them; they won't protect you like you protect them, so let them go. It's time.

Vulnerability is inevitable in this life. No matter how far I try to stay away from it, it finds me, and it will find you too. It isn't healthy to dodge your personal interactions and experience with hurt. It's such a huge part of how you live. Embrace and acknowledge the damage done because it's part of you.

Do you understand? It's painful; I know. It tugs at your heart; I know. But it is worth it. As DJ Khaled says, "Stay away from they!"

I say, stay away from those damn shades. The shades will get old. The shades will blind and bind you. The shades will make you weary.

Speak your truth.

The only people who will get angry at you for speaking the truth are those living a lie. Keep speaking it.

And for the record, I'm not okay, but I will be. Be aware that I am not easily broken.

CHAPTER 11

Time

If I could make time stand still, then I know we'd live
this moment forever. Can we stay right here?

—Cherish

Cherish these nights, cherish these people.
Life is a movie but there will never be a sequel.

—Nicki Minaj

Time: the indefinite continued progress of existence and
events in the past, present, and future regarded as a whole

Time, as it is defined above, is "indefinite," but we know that time on earth, for every individual, is limited.

From this point on, the content in my book gets closer to my heart. As I continue to write, my heart bleeds harder, and it's difficult to be vulnerable. I'll admit. It's terrifying to let my guard down, put my pride aside, and speak on my humiliation. Yet here I am. The nakedness of my soul is necessary—truly necessary.

We always seem to desire more time, but when granted, we waste most of it.

What does *time* mean to you? Does the dictionary definition have an impact on your interpretation of it? If you're unsure, that's cool; quite frankly, I'm still trying to make sense of it myself.

I will tell you, however, some of my conclusions, derived from personal experiences, on *time*.

First, you usually don't have as much time as you think you do. I don't think that any generation has known the value of time. This is a very tricky and unfortunate truth. Many of us don't need to rush to grow up, but we shouldn't stunt our growth either.

It's been said, that we have all the time in the world, but just not enough of it. Finding a happy medium seems nearly impossible. Figuring out the balance of time that suits our individual paths can be uncertain. Why? Because balancing time is not black or white; there's no bull's-eye, no set right or wrong answer.

Mentally and emotionally, many of us do not grasp the essence of time's subtle but potent treasures.

> Life teaches us to make good use of time, while
> time teaches us the value of life.
>
> —unknown

Will we ever know the true significance of time? Who knows? Maybe one day, maybe never. I know it's complex and probably beyond the ability of most human minds to comprehend, let alone to master.

Take procrastination, for instance. Procrastination is a weakness for many, especially college students, where *time* seems to always be there but never valued. But it was that very reality that made me want to take my time more seriously and to encourage others to do the same. Feel me?

Ask yourself the following questions:

- Why do I spend a lot of time worried about all the wrong things?

- Why do I get distracted so easily by the nonsense that society feeds me, letting time slip away?

I've asked myself why I've procrastinated on writing this memoir. Why have I wasted time and energy on things that do not serve me?

I think it discourages us when we have to actually think, when the reactions or outcomes we expect are not produced immediately. We slack off.

> If I knew, I was wastin' my time, would end up wastin'
> my time, with these shoulda, coulda, wouldas.
>
> —PartyNextDoor

> The way we spend our time defines who we are.
>
> —Jonathan Estrin

Remember: you always have "all the time in the world" until yours runs out ... and it will run out.

I've recently been conflicted over my views on time. My heart and mind have been very heavy leading up to the seventh anniversary of my grandmother's passing from breast cancer. The thoughts that run through my head are crazy. I'm constantly thinking of how the closest person to me is gone forever. It is the worst feeling; I wouldn't wish it on my worst enemy.

I went to visit her gravesite last week to clear my mind, and I couldn't believe how much time had gone by. I sat on the grass, looking in the sky, thinking, *It seems like yesterday you were here, Grandma. You were always excited for Christmas. You always reassured me that we weren't going to let cancer beat us and how strong we were in dealing with it. Now look where we are …*

It kills me to think that so much time passes, and I have no control over it. The only thing I can do is make the best of it, for her and the rest of my angels. Still, it's frustrating to have no control over time or what can happen in a millisecond.

My pastor, Anthony G. Maclin, said one Sunday, "When you give to God the very person you don't know how to live without, it touches the heart of heaven.

I hope I did significantly well with the task of touching the heart of heaven because the deaths of my grandma, my nana, my grandfather, and my cousin were very big chunks of the very thing I rely on to be—the one organ that keeps it all running, day in and day out, my heart.

I look around me and see my parents. I think of how long they've taken care of me and continuously have supported, advised, loved, and comforted me. The simple thought of their getting older (let alone any physical indication of it) *frightens* me to death.

There are only a few people for whom I would give my life, and my parents are, *without a doubt*, at the top of that list. While I'm excited to get older, to make it and to be working with the best of the best in various industries while experiencing new things, I never forget that time is passing.

Everything and everyone is aging around me, including me. My love for my parents and my sister is timeless, and God knows I would add more time to their clocks if it were possible. I can't lose them.

Time is what we want the most but use the worst.

—William Penn

Penn's quote is something we all can agree on. At one time or another in our lives, we have asked or yearned for more time. We all want it—that's evident—but I want you to think about it. If you were given more time, even a second more, how would you use it?

How would you apply it to make a significant difference in this life? Be honest with yourself.

The two most powerful warriors are patience and time.

—Leo Tolstoy

It is horrifying to not to know when it's someone's time to go; when it's your time to go. Truth be told, I can't fathom the thought of losing anyone else close to my heart. I will need someone's help if that happens, God forbid.

Time and patience have become my lifelong Band-Aids. They go hand in hand and have opened my eyes to a lot. I now see that events transpire to either shape me or break me. I was always taught that love and family would see me through, but I guess that was a lie. I don't understand it.

- Why do people claim they love you but go for months and years without speaking to you?

- How can people be so close to you one day and strangers the next, just a bad memory?

- How can "family" use you and use you until they can't anymore?

It bothers me. It confuses me. It tears me apart.

A lot of the things that I've gone through make me feel like I don't have a heart. Between the deaths in my family and getting hurt emotionally in friendships and situations, I don't see how I could *not* have a broken heart. Its being broken, for me, seemed inevitable, but then again, so did this book, and there's more to come.

God is intentional.

If I ever showed you (because I don't do much talking when it comes to expressing how I genuinely feel) that I love you, and I took time for you in my life, that was real. You can't ever knock what's real because it speaks for itself.

Of course we won't live forever on this earth. We are reminded every second that life is immeasurable but most of us treat it as useless.

It baffles me to think that I was created, only to live for a period, and then to leave again, like I never existed. Freaky. That alone should be incentive enough for you to value time.

Your time. Her time. His time. Their time. Our time.

Value and respect it; it will take you a long way. I hope you have the same epiphany as I had. The moment you realize how important time is, your entire perspective will change.

In loving memory of Josephine Allen (Sept. 5, 1932–Dec. 8, 2008)

Jeanette Goines (Nov. 23, 1941–April 14, 2018)

and the rest of my fallen Angels…

I love you. Everything I do is for you.

CHAPTER 12

Practice

It has taken practice for me to genuinely accept a compliment; to stop second-guessing myself; to not overthink every aspect of my life and my being; to realize we are not the same, and that's why I can't compare myself to you; to see that everyone is not built alike; to understand that not everything I want is necessarily good for me; and to enjoy the pace and direction of my life, as it is now.

> Never be in a hurry; do everything quietly and in a
> calm spirit. Do not lose your inner peace for anything
> whatsoever, even if your world seems upset.
>
> —thegoodquote

It has taken practice for me to *not* automatically assume that someone's intentions toward me were in my best interest; to stop questioning God about why my grandma couldn't beat cancer or why my cousin couldn't have dodged the bullet to his skull the night he was senselessly murdered; to stop blaming myself for people who willingly left my life at the worst times, it seemed; to realize that this is God's work.

I have to play the cards that I'm dealt, and I have to work overtime to make things happen, never giving up.

It has taken practice for me not to assume that everyone knows what I go through and cares about it; to know that I can't please everyone and can only live for me; to understand that a lot of people can't grasp how deep, real, and complex I am; to give myself credit for how far I've come.

It has taken practice for me to *not* define my current situation as my final destination.

I've concluded that if I didn't have the life I do now, I wouldn't have all this goodness to share with you. My writing wouldn't be as intriguing as it is.

As the saying goes, "Live life with no regrets." There are days, however, that I wish I could have a moment back to do things differently with and for some people.

This chapter was partially inspired by Kehlani's albums, *Cloud 19*, *You Should Be Here*, and *Sweet, Sexy, Savage*. After hearing her song "Get Away," I fell in love and was in tears, and I knew I had to buy them all. Her voice led me to a calm state. Lately, I've paid more attention to what artists feed me instrumentally, not just lyrically. Her most recent EP, *While We Wait*, was just the art I needed to realign, So I thank her for that. I don't support trash. Their music has to speak, move, and inspire me in some way for me to give it any attention.

We all need music at times to aid our mental escapes, and that's cool too. Temporary feelings are normal, but be careful not to get too attached to just feeling good in the moment. There are limits to what I'll support because it's a reflection of my morals and values.

I related to Kehlani because she told a true story and a raw story of who she was and is. She is multidimensional, as are all women. She paints vivid pictures of where she must go in life because of where she came from. I appreciate authenticity and humility in artists. When it's authentic, I can recognize it right off the bat, assuming they reflect the same qualities.

I connected to her pain, as I'm sure a lot of people have. It made me remember that not everyone given the label of "celebrity" identifies with that Hollywood notion; not everyone believes the hype. It takes *practice* to deal with the funny people—not just celebrities—you encounter in the world.

Kehlani is the same age as I am, and for her to have gone through what she's gone through and come out of it fiercer than ever is inspirational beyond measure.

I thank Kehlani for pouring her heart out through her impeccable voice and raw lyrics. Her testimony has not gone unnoticed, and I'm sure she has comforted and saved many lives with her truth, honesty, and vulnerability.

Honesty is bravery.

Transparency is bravery.

And it's something I want to make sure that I portray in my work all the time.

We should put transparency into practice because there's pureness in it. When I exercise it, no one can throw anything in my face that others don't already know about. No one can throw dirt on my name because I owned up to it all. No one can hurt me.

My credibility is visible for everyone to see. There is nothing for people to use to tear me down (except lies, which have never been relevant anyway). Unfortunately, that bothers devious, miserable people.

Embrace transparency. It takes practice to stay level-headed while dealing with everything people pull from left and right to discourage and discredit you. The test of faith, trust, and patience within myself and my work are the main obstacles that I must persevere through.

Keep practicing to prevail!

For those with a goal, dream, or idea, I need you to keep afloat! I know firsthand how challenging every day can be, but if you are destined to serve a purpose, then it's inevitable for your path. It will seem abnormal at first, but do not shy away from it.

Keep at it each day.

Whatever makes you and the world happy and then makes your world a better place, follow it.

Follow your feelings.

Your goosebumps,

The sensation that lives just outside of your skin and deep in your soul.

That's your yes.

And your yes matters.

Let it lead you in all you do.

—unknown

Keep singing, keep painting, keep dancing, keep writing, keep loving, and keep being passionate about what you love because the world needs you.

This thing called life takes practice. Remember: Harder paths equals higher callings.

If you don't practice, you don't deserve to win.

—Andre Agassi

Knowledge is a treasure, but practice is the key to it.

—Lao Tzu

Every rose needs rain sometimes.

CHAPTER 13

Unthinkable

The time has finally come. You made it. We made it. It's a bittersweet feeling, reaching this chapter of my life, but I'm grateful to have experienced it.

Everything I've shared to this point has been close to my heart, and what follows isn't any different.

It's one thing to be bound to someone emotionally because you share the same flesh or the same blood and bone. But it's a deeper and more intimate connection, mentally and emotionally, to be bound by the universe's doing.

As I've mentioned, I am fragile and sensitive. It's terrifying but a relief to tell my truth. I've been avoiding this chapter in particular. I've been ignoring these embedded thoughts. And this mental prison to which I'm constrained has been the most difficult to escape from.

Yet I need to share my story of *heartbreak*.

Some people may be surprised I've had heartbreak. Some may not know I was involved with anyone, while I imagine others saying, "I didn't know she had a heart to break," or "I didn't know that she felt anything, let alone felt so deeply."

That's idiotic. But whatever people think or say doesn't matter, not at this point, at least. (And I have forgiven their ignorance.) As long as this message gets to who it is intended for, *nothing else matters; no one else matters*. In this chapter, I want you to focus less on who is who and more on the lessons I learned—that's what's important.

This is my most naked, vulnerable, and pure state of being. Welcome to the part of life that everyone fails to talk about, as if it doesn't exist or hasn't touched them in any way. It's the lethal combination of fear, pain, and *love*.

This piece is my love; it's my heart that unraveled. I've learned that with such a true emotion that's so potent and spontaneous, the most *unthinkable* things will occur.

My pain was inevitable, but I was consciously, yet unconsciously, oblivious to it.

> The people that bring you the greatest pain in life also have
> the potential to bring you the greatest happiness.
>
> —@DavyJTheVirgo

So true.

I am not ashamed of my past. I was exclusively for one person. When you know that feeling, there almost are no limits to what you'll endure for love.

It's dangerous. It's risky. But it's the hopelessly romantic way.

I had never been in a serious, labeled, public "relationship" before this one. This was my first love, and our encounters have spread over more than nine years, as of this writing.

Some might classify the order in which things happened (or didn't happen) as backward, but I don't care. I didn't do it on purpose. God just had a plan, and it still is being carried out.

That's when I knew God had something serious in store for me.

To begin, I'm going to list every lesson I learned. I hope you'll think about each one—it will help you to understand. The lessons are as follows:

1. Know your worth.

2. Never settle.

3. Love yourself enough so that any other love simply adds to it.

4. You can tell a lot about a person by what he or she chooses to see in you.

5. Someone's perception of you is reflection of that person, and your reaction to that person is an awareness of you.

6. Don't let anyone define you by your past; everyone has one.

7. Forgive and be gentle with yourself.

8. Know which insecurities are yours and which are not.

9. People can only meet you as deeply as they've met themselves.

10. Protect your heart.

11. Be careful from whom you seek validation and acceptance because most people don't know what they want from themselves, let alone from you.

12. If it costs you your peace of mind, it's far too expensive.

13. You are the only one in control of your emotions.

14. Make sure your effort is matched 110 percent.

15. Don't put anything past anyone.

16. A woman will never be enough for a boy who is not ready.

17. You don't have to chase what God sent, and a lot of times he will put you through things just to show you that he is God.

18. Stop explaining yourself and justifying your character to others. They only understand from their level of perception.

19. You are not anything that makes you feel low in spirit.

20. Be with someone who is afraid of the *thought* of losing you and who is not scared to explore you; who accepts and wants all of you.

21. When I said I needed you, I didn't, but when I said I wanted you, I meant it, entirely.

The most beautiful part about loving a guarded girl is this: when she lets you in, it's not because she needs you. She stopped needing people a long time ago. It's because she wants you. And that is the purest love of all.

In this long list, I'd say trust and forgiveness played the biggest roles in what I dealt with. I had to forgive so that I could be free and be okay.

Forgiveness doesn't mean reentry. Just because I forgive you doesn't mean that we should try again, nor does it mean that we will be in each other's lives again. Forgiveness is solely for me—for my peace of mind, my sanity. It's for me to be okay with the fact that what is meant for me will always be for me.

I had to believe this was true for me, that it applied to me and wasn't just a fairy-tale idea that wasn't attainable. And when I did begin to believe, it made thinking about all the madness easier to endure because, ultimately, God was in control.

Nine times out of ten, when I stress, it derives from overthinking or overly obsessing on an idea or topic that I want to let go. Things that can't change and things over which I have no control gotta go.

Note to self: to hold on is a waste of energy.

Preserve your energy.

Protect your heart.

PART 1

His Pursuit

It began in my freshman year of high school. As I've mentioned, I was shy, but as the year went on, I became more comfortable and confident. The last thing on my mind was taking anyone seriously. I was just looking for friends, and luckily, I found one in him.

We became friends, and our friendship was innocent and pure. We had good conversations, although I still kept to myself when we met. He had a girlfriend, and I was chillin' anyway, so it all worked out. We talked about just about everything, and he found out that I was "crazy," which he liked, so that also worked out.

When he started to have romantic feelings for me, he wasn't the one who expressed it to me. No, a mutual friend, who had her nose in everyone's business but her own, beat him to the punch.

My own feelings for him started to grow the more we talked, which became a daily and nightly thing. Before I knew it, he had broken up with his girlfriend—I was shocked, but I had nothing to do with that. I found out about his break-up from our mutual friend during tumbling practice. She said he broke up with her for me.

I hadn't asked him to do that, so part of me felt bad, even though he claimed I wasn't the reason. (But it also didn't seem like a coincidence either.)

And so we started speaking to each other even more. He eventually told me why he broke up with his ex, but it didn't matter at that point—other than to stress the point that my coming between them wasn't my intention. (I didn't need any bad karma.) And now that he was unattached, I suppose we were "dating," whatever that means at the age of fourteen.

I had an eventful freshman year at Bowie High School—including meeting my high school sweetheart—and now I was ready to tackle sophomore year, which was a transition year. It was a big deal. I was still trying to find myself, but I had moved to the main building—the freshmen were separated from the rest of the school, as they had all their classes in annex, which was right up the street from the main building. As a sophomore, it was a rush to be with all the other classes during the day. I felt that this year was *it*. I would show off and show out because I was in the building with the seniors, and I wasn't a rookie anymore.

I had shop for a new wardrobe. I had to make sure I dressed up every day for class. And I had to make sure that I wore the shortest shorts for cheer practice, as the guys would conveniently walk through the cafeteria during that time, even though they weren't supposed to. I wasn't fast like that, although many on my team were. I, however, was a virgin. I was even scared to kiss him (or anyone). I was reserved and still so immature that kissing seemed "nasty" to me. (I thought, *Swapping spit with another human being? Gross! I'll pass!*) I was just a baby, and I wasn't ready.

I also was self-conscious, and because I knew he told his loudmouth best friend (our mutual friend) *everything*, I didn't want him saying anything about me that was foul. (It bothered me that he told her everything; I felt *I* should have been his best friend in that sense. I should have nipped that relationship in the bud, but I kept quiet.) Bottom line—at least for me at that age—was that boys had cooties.

He was a gentleman and never made me feel weird for how I felt. He never pressured me to do anything. That was a plus. At this point, he seemed selfless and sincere. Our relationship was based on genuine vibes and long conversations. We talked about nothing and sometimes about everything.

I wanted to learn a lot from him because, in my eyes, he knew how to do so much, and I admired that about him.

He was talented in the arts and sports, which was a major plus for me. From the drums, to the piano, singing, skating, and golfing, he was versatile when it came to things of that nature, and it intrigued me. That was because I appreciated diversity, so I identified more and more with him and unconsciously began to grow closer to him.

I asked him to teach me to play the piano, to golf, and to roller skate. He agreed but then never taught me the piano because he thought he couldn't play very well. I thought he was being modest; I only cared that he knew more than I did, and I was open to learning new things.

He was genuinely interested in me, as I was in him, and before I knew it, our casual conversations became sincere expressions of *I love you, I miss you,* and *I want you.*

I know now it was puppy love, but it was real for us, and that's the scary part. We called each other cute nicknames. We had our own song ("Unthinkable" by Alicia Keys), and we made a lot of memories that meant a lot to me. It felt really good to have someone in touch with me, the way I was with him, with hardly any effort.

There was a natural *pull* between us. It all was perfect—too perfect; almost too good to be true.

As we got closer to the point where he felt things could go to the next level, that's when I began to freeze. It was like my feelings were placed on halt because I didn't know what the "next level" would bring. I had a fear of the unknown when it came to my heart and my love. I had anxiety attacks over it, and the worst possible thoughts went through my mind. I had doubts, and I suddenly expected to be let down. I thought that we weren't going to work out. I was scared out of my mind, although I didn't recognize it as such at the time.

I thought that we were moving a bit fast, but I didn't communicate that. I started to question if he was who I thought he was, or if things would change as soon we made it official.

Was he who I really wanted? I didn't know. I kept that to myself. I kept brushing it off like it was nothing and like the feeling would pass. I had thoughts of breaking it off with him, trying to prevent my being hurt.

At fifteen, of course I didn't understand the concept of fighting for love or the concept of love, really. I didn't know how rare it was to have someone who genuinely cared about me, my mind, my body, and my soul—and vice versa. I'm not justifying my actions or downplaying his pain from what I decided to do next. That's just how it was, and that's the beauty of truth.

I kept a lot to myself and felt myself pulling away from him, and that freaked me out. I'd ask myself what was wrong with me. *You were just so in love, and now you're switching up for what?* Since I wasn't sure what was up, I needed to vent, and like an idiot, I expressed my feelings to our mutual friend.

I'd like to think I confided in her because she knew him much better than I did, but it hurt me to admit that. (How can you force someone to let you in? Answer: you can't.) The petty side of me wondered what he was telling her that he couldn't tell me.

I confided in her because I was confident she had the best insight on what I should do. And she did, surprisingly. She told me to keep talking to him because he really loved me, and he hadn't tried anything yet that would give me a reason to abruptly pull away. I was just being paranoid.

And for once, she was absolutely right. Too bad that mattered when it was already too late.

Those were the facts, but I didn't listen.

Sometimes I wish I could've gone to my parents, but we didn't have that type of relationship. I don't fault them for that, but it would've been nice.

I was young and dumb, however, and our mutual friend became the third person in my and his relationship. Allowing her to have that role was the worst decision of my life.

It was our annual class night, when each class does a performance in preparation for homecoming. As a sophomore and a cheerleader, I had to do a performance with my squad. Before that night, however, I felt off all day, and I felt like I had to tell him that we would be best as just friends. I texted him, saying only that we needed to talk. When he called me later, we made small talk (which I hate), and then I just blurted the words: "I don't think we should talk anymore. I think that we should just be friends. Don't hate me."

There was dead silence from him for what seemed like several minutes. I kept saying things that I hoped would lighten the moment, as if that were possible, because I just had shattered his heart to pieces. "I don't want you to hate me," I told him. "Please don't be mad at me. I still want us to be friends."

When he finally spoke, it was in the quietest voice, possibly to keep himself from crying while on the phone with me. Obviously, I was the least liked person that night, but I felt like a weight had been lifted (temporarily) because *in my head*, I had guaranteed that I wasn't going to get hurt. Or so I thought. As I've mentioned, I was young and dumb.

If you let fear hold you back, you'll never be able to move forward.

—Seema Bansal

He said that he wasn't mad at me, and he didn't hate me. I knew his heart was broken, but I couldn't feel it. I couldn't feel, period. It was like I went stone cold. I was numb. I was a child, and my actions showed it, but I carried on.

The next day at school, I saw him in the hallway, and he looked so depressed. Of course, everyone knew about us within twenty-four hours (I wonder who told them). People came up to me, asking if I'd seen him that day. They said he looked sad or like he had been crying. That didn't make me happy, but at the same time, everyone's "concern" was a bit much, a bit overwhelming.

It wasn't that I wanted him to hurt; I obviously didn't. But I also didn't want to force myself to be with someone because that's what he and everyone else wanted. I wasn't the yes-man anymore. I'd put my foot down.

Yet there was always a part of me, especially when I looked into his eyes, that knew I had royally messed up—but I ignored it. I was being very selfish, but I told people, "It's not my fault that these are my feelings. I can't force something if it's not what I want." And I believed that. To a certain extent that was true—but not entirely.

I felt like I had to justify my choice, so I started pulling things out of the woodwork, and even I knew I was reaching. For instance, sometimes our mutual friend would tell me what he thought of other girls or what he thought of the girls on our cheer team. I felt like I was pushed to the side for others. Whether she knew it or not, which she probably did, her unsolicited comments really messed with me.

I came up with every excuse so that I wouldn't look like the bad guy. (From my standpoint, I didn't think I was.) My self-esteem was a serious issue. I thought I was ugly and fat through most of my high school years. I wouldn't say anything, but it was all recorded in my head. I compared myself to others and was jealous of my friends for that reason. Our mutual friend told me random comments he'd made about other girls, and I just didn't fit the script. I thought he was better off without me and that I was doing both of us a favor by leaving him alone.

Later that day, I ran into him. I still remember exactly what he was wearing—an olive-green sweatshirt with a black hood, and sunglasses.

When I saw him, my heart instantaneously dropped. I immediately felt terrible inside because seeing his sad face really broke me. Yet I didn't let that show, and that wasn't easy. I kept telling myself he'd get over it; that I had made *the right decision.*

I walked up to him, and minimal words were exchanged, though none needed to be. The body language and the intense gaze from his eyes said enough. I told him to give me a hug, and he reluctantly did. It was faint but warm at the same time; as if I'd taken everything out of him with just that one touch. I looked into his big brown eyes but not for too long. Then, as I pulled back, he looked like he was holding back the heaviest tears. He was making me so sad, and I told him to smile. I didn't want to see him like that, but there was nothing I could do. So I turned and walked away.

Late that night, as I was getting ready for bed, I felt fine but also a little guilty. I tried not to dwell on that or join everyone in making me feel bad. So I said my prayers. I lay my head down and fell into a deep sleep.

When I woke up the next morning, the first thing I did was check my phone. He'd sent a text in the middle of the night that simply read: "Chántelle."

That was it.

I responded right away. I thought something was wrong, like he was in trouble, or he just wanted to talk, but he never replied after that.

I didn't realize he'd been uncontrollably reaching for me; trying to pull me back in; trying to get me to realize that I didn't have to run away from him or fear what I didn't know.

But I didn't get it. I just didn't. Or I didn't want to.

By the time I was sixteen, I started entertaining other people. These were stupid little boys who I thought I wanted and who I believed were "cool" or socially acceptable. Throughout this phase of my life, he and I were cordial. He never shut me out like I expected. I knew if I ever needed anything, I could reach out to him, and vice versa. He wore his heart on his sleeve, no matter what, and I loved that about him.

We saw each other in passing a lot, and toward junior year, things seemed good. We were genuine friends who loved one another from a distance.

By this time, he had a girlfriend. I still was in the stage of finding and appreciating myself, so I was doing my own thing. Yet I couldn't help but notice that every time he and I were in the same room, there was always a big elephant with us. You couldn't have paid me to address that, however. I kept ignoring it because I didn't think he was interested in me anymore; I thought our time was done.

I sometimes thought about the possibility of rekindling a romance, but I left it as a thought.

By senior year, I was starting to identify which people were who they said they were. At this time, our mutual friend was now less of a friend. She and I had falling apart, and so did they. I don't know why they stopped being "best friends"; I suppose they just grew apart. He didn't seem to think anything of it and was still cordial to her, but she took it hard and was upset about their fall-out.

Every time she and I were together, his name came up, and she would tell me all about his business (like who he was having sex with, who he messed around with), although I never asked for that information. I didn't know if she wanted me to look at him funny and stop talking to him as well, but it seemed she never failed to throw dirt on his name around me.

It seemed to me that feelings were there between them. I don't know whether it was from him or her or both, but it didn't sit right with me then, and it never will.

PART 2

My Pursuit

High school was now old news, and I showed up and showed out in my graduating class of 2013. I enjoyed my summer, carefree and semi-stress-free. It all led me to the next big step: college.

Freshman year was my best year as far as having genuine fun, freedom, and peace of mind. I entered with a clean slate, but it wasn't too long after I'd decided to keep my distance from this boy that he somehow found his way back into my life.

I was lying on my bed in my cute, quaint but ancient dorm room, listening to music. I had been getting to know my first roommate. (I had two roommates. I had a habit of driving away the energy that doesn't vibe with me. I admire that quality in me.) After we finished our conversation, I was scrolling on Instagram, and out of nowhere, I started getting notifications of "likes" on my pictures. I checked on who it was, and it was him.

I got excited when I saw his name. I clicked on his page and looked to see what he'd been up to since graduation. Then I decided to text him.

He replied instantly.

And just like that, our connection was restored. Back like we'd never left.

From that point on, we texted more frequently. He was genuine in his interactions with me, and so was I with him. One night, we were on

Facetime, and I was telling him about my concerns with studying abroad and finding another church home. He reassured me that everything would work out if it was God's will for me to go abroad. Regarding church, he offered to take me the next time I came home for a weekend.

I needed to find a church home that I liked and could relate with more than the one I'd grown up in. Plus, I just wanted to see him, and what better place to reunite than in the house of the Lord?

Coincidentally, I'd already planned to go home the following weekend. When I did, I went to his church. I fell in love with everything about it because it advocated having a relationship with God, as opposed to having a religion with him. I was grateful to have that experience, but unfortunately, it led us into a space where I was the only one bound, emotionally and mentally, once again.

Nothing was established between us, but I told him how I felt about him. He, however, was the most hesitant about me but still felt deeply for me. Weird, I know. It was complicated, I guess.

It was more than obvious that this was more than just a friendship; it had stopped being just a friendship back in ninth grade.

My freshman year at college ended, and I was home for the summer. I am a summer baby, and in July, I had my annual birthday pool party. I was turning nineteen, but it wasn't a big deal. This year I didn't want a big party because I was gravitating away from certain people, habits, and atmospheres, but I still had one. I made the mistake of inviting people I didn't care for; most of them are irrelevant now.

Remember that he and I were in a weird place of strong feelings and attachment. Even though he was nonchalant about me and us, I invited him. I wanted him to come. Little did I know that this party would start something that would leave memories of joy and pain *all over again.* There are permanent scars on my heart. I partially did it to myself, but that's how the cookie crumbled, I guess.

Being around him just made me want him more and more. After that night, he came over to my house a lot. We spent a lot time together. One time when he came over, we had a conversation—I don't remember exactly how it started—that included my addressing the question of what we were doing.

"Why do you act like you don't care if we speak, or you act mean if I want to talk to you all the time?" I asked. "I don't want to feel like I'm doing too much, but you say one thing and then act another way as soon as we are apart. Again, I need to know what are we are doing." After gaining courage with those comments, I just threw out, "I want us to be together."

I was a fool to think it would be that easy. "I want to be more than your friend," I said. "I want to be with you, and I don't see why it's not that easy."

I still didn't understand the damage I (and whoever else) had done to him. I thought that enough time had passed and that we were ready to take that route with one another, which never had been fully pursued. I thought it was a great idea to give it another shot.

When I said all of that, he was quiet for a minute. Then, while laughing, he said, "You want to know something?"

"What?"

"I'm scared of you."

At the time, I thought he was joking. Back then, I didn't know what he meant by that.

Today, I do!

My instant reaction was the sincerely confused, "What exactly do you mean you're scared of me, boy?"

"I'm scared of your being wishy-washy and indecisive; your ability to get me so deep into you and then picking up and leaving because one day you change your mind about us. I'm scared we wouldn't work, and if I fall, you wouldn't catch me—for the second time."

Now I got it. It was then that I realized how much I had hurt him. I'd known all along that his pain was real, but he never showed it. He got into a relationship right after we broke things off, so I thought everything was cool. I didn't think he cared about me or what we'd had.

When he said this, I knew he was being dead serious. I also sensed that the thought of our being together had definitely crossed his mind, maybe more than I thought it had. Yet that legitimate fear was clearly greater than his desire to pursue us. Even when I realized that, though, I kept pushing. Because you fight for what you want, right?

After that conversation, I was mentally drained. I didn't really understand what was going on with us. This haze of a feeling became the norm, and in the future, we had multiple "serious talks." We still talked regularly, as if dating was still on the table. That's obviously what I wanted, so I went with the flow. I thought that just giving him time to become more vulnerable, without pushing the topic, was the unspoken answer. Eventually, things would fall into place.

At least, that's what I thought would happen. The ball was in his court. That was a mistake.

With the temporary joy of the idea we were working toward something came overwhelming confusion and uncertainty. This then translated into stressing over someone who wasn't mine—which he made super-clear at his earliest convenience.

Some days things would be good, but then I would get an attitude about something he did. I can be petty, and I get mad when I don't get my way. I now know that that's no way to behave in a relationship, but I didn't know that then.

When I'd get mad, I'd throw a tantrum or act like I didn't care; I'd let my pride get the best of me. Men rely on pride by default, so that was a deadly recipe for any growth. Usually, when I'd acted that way in the past, it had worked, in the sense that I would let pride win. I genuinely would not care about the guy, and he'd blow up my phone, and then we would start talking again. Childish, I know.

But this time around, it was different.

I cared.

I cared deeply.

And this time, I couldn't help it.

It was as if I unconsciously became in sync with his every move. Everything he did or said affected me, and I took it to heart. That was the last thing my emotional self needed—that moment when you care for another's being more than you do for yours.

I had to adjust.

I wasn't used to someone telling me about myself and caring. When I threw my fits, he would say that I needed to work on my "consistency." I think this is where my attitude and my struggle with communication came into play as well.

Usually, if someone would tell me I need to work on something, my immediate response would be to tell that person to get lost because I wasn't changing for anyone.

But with him, I wanted to work on myself so we could work. I definitely wanted to do it for the wrong reason, but he made me want to be better, all in all.

I thought, *If this is something that I want to build with him, then why not give it a go?*

It was rare, and it was real, so I had to put in my best effort. I began to see it from a different angle. Since people don't necessarily change but rather improve, I was going to work on improving myself. That was the goal, regardless, so it wasn't a negative thing at all.

It was supposed to be more for me than for him, but this time I knew that I needed to not just *say*, "I am trying to change," but act on it. I could feel that I was somewhat, on thin ice with him; he didn't believe that I wanted us to be together, so I started to focus on improving me.

When you want someone and something so bad, you work hard for it—sometimes, at all costs.

Yet with me putting this work in, I also let him know that it wasn't going to fly for him to treat me like I was anything like one of those other girls he talked to or who threw themselves at him. I felt that I wasn't getting the attention or respect that I needed, and I was getting restless. I also informed him that he was not perfect either. If we were going to try anything, then effort needed to be matched across the board.

What wasn't going to work? Just the following:

- A nonchalant attitude

- Replying whenever he wanted

- Joking about anything that wasn't funny

- Being disrespectful

- Throwing my past in my face

- Making excuses for not trusting and not being vulnerable

- Picking and choosing when he wanted to show his love for me

- Treating me as a convenience, not a priority

I don't think he understood that I would never put in that much effort into anyone else. I didn't like being told what to do, and I was working with him.

Stupid.

I have a confession: at one time, I couldn't (or was not willing to) communicate my true feelings very well with others. It takes a lot for me to get mad, but when it all comes out, it all comes out full force! They say that to fully move on, you have to leave past habits and past issues behind. So that's what I proceeded to do, but there were two people in this thing.

It could all be so simple

But you'd rather make it hard

Loving you is like a battle

And we both end up with scars

Tell me, who I have to be

To get some reciprocity

No one loves you more than me

And no one ever will

—Lauryn Hill, "Ex-Factor"

I'm someone who likes to nurture. I care if you ate today. I care how your day was. I want to know what's on your mind and want to feel your energy. ("How's your heart baby? What are plans to expand in the future?")

For some, that's "too much" or "too deep."

No such thing with me.

I will love you to no end. I'll always see the good in you and your potential before anything else, most of the time. My character speaks for itself; that's just who I am. My love is sweet, profound, and refreshing.

Didn't he know this? Clearly, he didn't.

We started officially "dating" toward the end of summer before my sophomore year. He told me we could take things slow. By this time, I felt more vulnerable than I should've been with him. No matter what anyone said, a part of me felt like I owed that to him.

On August 14, 2015, a week before I left to go back to school, I kissed him for the first time. (Whoo-oooo!) It was so cute and romantic.

We were sitting in his car, and he was getting on my nerves because he loved to say silly things without thinking, and we started play-fighting. Next thing I knew, he was holding my face in his hands. We were super-close, and it was awkward for me to get that close to someone, especially when I had feelings for him.

We looked into each other's eyes. He hesitated for a second, and then it just happened. He pressed his full, soft, plush lips against mine, and I returned the favor—very innocent, gentle, and endearing.

At the time, it felt like magic. If I've known it in this lifetime, that's how I would describe it. When we pulled back, realizing that that was the first time we'd expressed our love physically, we started laughing. It was cute; I won't lie.

He said, "You know that was our first time kissing because you wanted to be a butthole and not kiss me in high school."

I just burst out laughing. "Yes, I know."

"I was scared to kiss you just now."

"Why?"

"I didn't know how I was going to feel. I was scared that I would feel everything that I tried to bury about you. I don't know why I'm so attached to you."

I was so confused, but I just wanted it to work, so I let it be.

The next week, I saw him right before I went back to school, and we talked about how things would with our dating, considering our distance. I told him I did not do long-distance relationships, and he agreed.

And that was the end of the story. It was over but fun while it lasted.

No, it could never be that simple, although I wish it could.

I returned to Philly, and the semester was now in full force. I had tests, homework assignments, and quizzes nearly every day. And I talked to him every day ... or at least every other day.

For about a month, things were cool, but then I got that dreadful feeling of things being too good to be true. The shenanigans started up again in September.

Something I forgot to mention: From the time I left for school until mid-September, we argued and disagreed often. It seemed we were never on the same page. He always complained about me. He never had anything positive to say about me. Part of our misunderstanding of one another was that he insisted on holding back and being immature, while I was putting in my everything. He was always joking and never took anything seriously. He never put me first—yes, I compared my place to his best friend or his other friends or "sisters." It seemed I wasn't important to him—if I was, he never showed it. And it bothered me that I was his significant other, yet he endlessly talked about other women all the time.

I felt like I could be secure—until it was obvious that it was something different. Until it was obvious that he'd rather be elsewhere. I felt like I always came second, third, last—everything *but* first—to one of his female friends, and I was not okay with that at all, especially as I put everyone in my circle second to him. I forgot who I was for a minute.

I hate the number two, that shit is unforgiven.

—Drake

My motto was to become, "Match my effort, or get away from me."

Yet for far too long, I allowed it. And so it continued.

In mid-September, the first major decline in this roller coaster occurred. One day we were texting, and out of the blue, he said, "Are you talking to me in the hope that we will be something in the future? Or no matter what we end up being, do you still want to be in my life as my friend?"

I hated getting messages like that. My stomach dropped when I read those words, and I thought, *What the hell are you talking about? One minute you want to talk to me, and the next you aren't ready, and you need time. Then you're just completely backing out.* It was too much. Meanwhile, my heart was wide open and exposed.

I responded, "I guess I want to be in your life as your friend, regardless, but why? Where is this question coming from?" Actually, I thought, *Am I strong enough or willing—no, is it even possible for us to just be friends? No. It isn't.*

He replied, "Because I just realized that I'll never be able to be vulnerable with you again. I don't trust you. I feel like if I told you something in confidence while we were on good terms, you would use it against me if we fell out. We don't understand one another. I feel like we just don't get along. I also think that right now, you don't possess the qualities that I need you to have for us to move forward."

He wrote a whole bunch of other BS that makes me angry all over again as I relive this. I'm angry for me back then too because I remember exactly how I felt as I write this. He was taking shots at my character. He couldn't claim he knew me and then hit me with that mess. If that's how he felt about me or how he described me others, including his family, then that was an issue. That's a *foul*.

They throwin' dirt on my old name.

—Drake

I sat there staring at my phone, wondering what was happening. I defended myself, of course. I gave him reasons why he should be vulnerable with me again (although I didn't need to prove myself to anyone). I added my thoughts on his being spiteful and selfish, seriously asking me to just be his friend.

Idiot, I thought. *I am not my mistakes. Stop throwing it in my face.*

I felt he wasn't seeing me for me but through the lens of how I broke his heart, and it wasn't fair.

People can only meet you as far as they've met themselves.

Is it your fears, that cause you to switch gears?

How do you hit the brakes before it ever starts?

I see you.

I see you.

For the man that you are and for the man you could be.

I see you, but do you see me?

I just want to know.

—Chóntel Carrington

I should have left him right there. He then said that was how he felt, and it was my decision if I wanted to speak with him as a friend or not, but he was serious.

"Okay, cool. We will be friends," I said.

I thought I could change his mind. I still had *hope*.

When I wasn't with him, it appeared easy for him to turn off his feelings. He denied that it was "easy," but it was done, and that's what counted.

After we established that "friends" was obviously best, I was chillin'. In October, although we were strictly friends now, he still tried it, as a guy would. He still told me he loved me and tried to throw in cute names here and there. He would allude to things, suggesting that he cared, but I knew better. He was all talk. I told him that he could not play with my feelings, but then I still let him. I pulled a "him" on him but ended up screwing myself over. I was totally convinced that I was going to change his mind. They say love conquers all. Yeah, we'll see.

We talked every day, until one day, out of the blue again, he decided to go missing. I didn't hear from him for about three weeks. Reluctantly, I texted him: "What's up? I haven't heard from you. Did I do something?"

He said that he needed a *break*.

I wondered how he could need a "break" from a friend. I thought, *Boy, we aren't even in the same state. How much more space do you need? Am I smothering you? Am I that bad?*

If that was the case, he should have said so. I didn't have time to guess. I didn't have time for games or jokes.

Yet despite how I felt about this "break," I let him have his time. I believe in giving people the time they ask for, no matter if it makes sense to me or not. My deepest fear was pushing him away because I was doing too much or loving him too hard—even though it's not possible in my world to love someone too hard. In my eyes, he had to be in a position to reciprocate my energy.

When he finally contacted me again, it was around the time that I was going home for the weekend, which was convenient because we'd made plans—prior to his randomly distancing himself from me—to link. As if going for weeks without talking to him wasn't enough punishment, however, he then decided to get on my nerves the day I came home. Amazing!

I don't even remember what it was; it was always something with him. It was always one complaint after the next. I can guarantee, however, that it was stupid. As it turned out, I didn't see him that entire weekend. I hadn't seen him since August, and this was late October. Clearly, I was the only one who cared about that.

Why didn't I see him? Because he didn't reply to me for most of that day and then gave me dry responses when he eventually did reply. The next day, he stayed out with his amazing friends. Clearly, I wasn't important. He hadn't seen me in three months but acted dumb when I came home. He was more concerned with spending time with the people he saw weekly and sometimes daily. Okay.

People make time for what and who they want. End of story.

Moreover, this boy had the audacity to not only go to see one of his female friends on the day we were supposed to link up, but he also bought her a pair of shoes and flowers—and God knows what else—for her birthday.

I thought, *I'm through,* and *I'm about to lose it.*

I find it difficult to find the words to describe how I felt. I was completely baffled and utterly annoyed. Why was he so disrespectful? Why didn't he see an issue with that?

I didn't get it. He had told me that he'd canceled whatever he had to do that weekend so he could see me. That's what he'd told me—and then you didn't follow through.

I felt such incredible rage. My insides were churning because of his stupidity, selfishness, and stubbornness. As I mentioned, I didn't see him that weekend. I sent him a message on Sunday, though, telling him that I'd seen where his priorities were and that he was foul for lying to me and not even trying to see me. I ended that message with, "I'm done."

His only response was, "Okay."

And we left it at that. Outraged but also sad, I didn't reply.

I went home that night and vented to my best friend; I was just in an all-around bad mood.

Three weeks went by, and neither of us reached out to the other. I followed him on social media, so I did my daily check-ins, and I'm sure he was checking on me as well, whether he'd admit it or not.

I saw that he was "having it up" with all his friends, and that was his business. I was hurt, of course. It wasn't a good feeling to know that I wouldn't ever come first with him, especially because I wouldn't have hesitated to prioritize him. But I also didn't think that our relationship was actually *done*. I thought he was just being an ass, as usual, and that he would come to his senses sooner or later.

My mistake.

By November, I had grown even more emotionally unstable because I was allowing the fact that we weren't speaking to get to me. It was an emotional roller coaster to deal with him. I was going crazy, asking myself about his actions, but I didn't have any answers.

Most people hate to get the message, "We need to talk." So considering that, I decided to write down my feelings down instead of trying to talk to him. I needed to map everything out and have a strategic plan this time around.

When I was finished, I was sure my message had broken records for number of pages. I wrote him a fourteen-page letter, letting him have everything left in me. It hit on a number of different points, including the following:

- He chose to see my weaknesses instead of my strengths, which reflected some of his own insecurities (in my opinion).

- His second-guessing and his uncertainty was clear, as if I hadn't been with him for the past seven months while he was uncertain about me.

- He didn't accept me for who I was in my entirety.

- He should realize that my coming back into his life meant something.

- I wasn't here because I wanted to put on a show or show everyone. I was doing what felt right in my spirit, and I was genuine in every move that I made.

While writing that message, I seriously tried to figure out how we had gotten to where we were. especially because I knew that he clearly loved me. One day he called me to say that he'd planned to tell me he didn't want to talk to me anymore, but then when he heard my voice, he changed his mind.

Things like that touched me, deeply, but at the same time, they were mind games. It was like he was in a constant battle between his heart and his mind. He would say things like, "I have to talk to you about something important, but I'm not sure if we should talk about it yet. I'm going to wait."

Excuse me? I think not. Stop messing with me and say what you want to say. That's what I wanted to say each time he did that. But I'd learned life is a cycle, and that was my karma. It was time for that love to come back around. That's how I knew it was real.

I sometimes think I was crazy to write a fourteen-page message to him. And I was—crazy in love.

I cannot put into words how I felt as I waited in confusion and pain after I sent the message. I never had feelings for anyone else where I thought about him every second. I cared for his well-being before acknowledging any of his flaws. It was *soul recognition*; I am more than positive.

One question I kept asking myself—and still ask to this day—is, "Would you fight for me the way I fought for you?"

My best friend, who felt my unbearable urge to talk to him when I explained what had occurred in the past three weeks, carefully considered everything I said. Together we planned to see where his head was because she could tell I was very adamant about him in general and making things work.

Next thing I knew, I was relaxing in my apartment, making dinner, when I got a text from my best friend: "Today is going to be a good day."

I had a feeling what she was referring to, but I didn't ask.

About four hours later, I got a text from him … and things took a turn for the worst. We made small talk in text messages, and then he stopped replying.

I was waiting for him to reach out in what seemed, at first, to be a comforting breath of fresh air—and it suddenly was the complete opposite. I knew something was up, and I couldn't shake the feeling. Meanwhile, my best friend was texting with both of us, and she relayed to me her entire conversation with him.

Suddenly, I got the text that I always dreaded getting from her: "Leave him alone. He just blew me."

Why? My stomach dropped, and I wondered what she was about to tell me. *It has to be another girl*, I thought. *It has to be. I know it is.*

And sure enough, it was ... because men are dirty, predictable, and usually only think with one thing.

When you need to find out something about your "man," your best friend should be down to do the dirty work, to find out if all the snooping is even worth it. Unfortunately, that night I found out that it wasn't.

They had a conversation in which he told her that he was "barely talking" to another girl, and he didn't know who he should talk to.

This was another sign. Three weeks had gone by, and he hadn't cared enough to fix anything with me, and he didn't think twice about moving on to the next woman. *Why am I here?* I thought. *You're not for me. Why do I want you? If I'm so disposable and replaceable to you, what makes me want you so bad?*

He insisted that it was nothing serious, and that if he "decided" (another red flag— the ball should always be in your court, ladies, always!) to talk to me, he would definitely stop talking to the other girl because he would never talk to someone else while he was talking to me.

There were many things wrong with that picture, and so I needed a drink. This boy ended up calling me, and I had to numb all the emotions that came with him, every last one. I explained how I felt about everything, from the weekend that he bailed on me until that very moment. We agreed on some things and disagreed on others.

I told him the reason we were on the phone was to figure out what we were. He said he couldn't give me an answer, so again I gave him more time. I gave him the opportunity to tell me he wanted me to leave him alone. He wasn't getting anything from me physically. "Just tell me you don't want me, that you want nothing to do with me, and I'll let you be." He could never say it.

He knew I would do it. It would've been hard, but I'm a strong woman, and I'd have pushed through.

> A deep woman only knows how to love deep. If you can't love her
> deeply, she will walk away. She doesn't know how to casually date
> someone she's really into or be friends with someone she has feelings for.

> —Rania Naim

I told him, "Just so we are very clear, if you choose not to pursue me, then we won't be friends. We won't be anything because I love you, and that will be too hard—damn near impossible for me to do. You know that from firsthand experience. I know I've told you that I wanted to be in your life regardless, but that was before I came to grips with how deep my love is for you. You've told me that you see my potential and that you could see yourself falling in love with me, see yourself marrying me, and even having kids with me, but then you're at a stalemate when we have the best opportunity to just build. I don't get it."

He responded in awe over the less important aspects, like the fact that I would delete him from social media and delete his number ... foolish boy.

I knew that I had to protect me because being with him and having anxiety over his uncertainty would do a lot more damage to me in the long run. I couldn't force it anymore.

"So if I see you in public somewhere, and you see me, should I speak, or are you going to ignore me? I just need to know now so I know how to act."

"Speak," I told him, "but leave it at that. No hug, no smile. Maybe you'll get a what's-up, but if not, just a head nod, and go on about your business. Depending on the day, however, I could walk right past you too, like we never met."

146

"Wow."

"Yup, it sucks, I know, but that's what you'll be asking for, sir. I won't allow you to have your cake and eat it too anymore, while you sit there and hold my past actions over my head and use that as an excuse for why you can't see me for the person I am and who I am becoming. I won't allow you to see me for me, only when it is convenient for you."

Nope, not going to happen!

> We all have good and bad inside of us. It's what side we
> choose to follow that defines who we really are.
>
> —J. K. Rowling

He still claimed that he wasn't judging me by my past, but he was.

I said, "You haven't forgiven me for not wanting to talk to you freshman year and how I broke your heart and disregarded your feelings—"

"Okay," he interrupted, "I don't want to talk about it. Can we not talk about it?"

I froze and said okay, fine. That just confirmed my comment about my past. I thought he was over it, but I'd clearly hit a nerve, a wound in his heart that had not healed.

Fact: Guys take it worse when they get hurt. They are more emotional beings than females are.

How could I think that we would build toward anything greater if he couldn't even talk about the damage that was done. I didn't see how I'd overlooked that piece, but then again, I strongly believe that love overrides every doubt that pain and anger could ever bring.

So I gave him more time to figure out whatever he needed to figure out, but I was conflicted. Should I have given him that much leeway?

He knew that this "choice" was not a game; it was final.

If you can't or don't want to be with me at my worst, then you don't deserve to have me at my best.

Meanwhile, I was internally trying to prepare for cutting him off. I refused to swallow my words (prideful, I know). I had to be fair to my heart, though, and I didn't want him to be in a situation where he wasn't happy and was just saying he wanted to be with me because he knew that's what I really wanted.

That would be chaotic turmoil for both of us.

As it got close to Christmas time, my favorite time of the year, and I was home for the holidays, I kept asking him if he'd decided. Of course, he kept giving me the run-around, but I took that as a good thing.

I thought, *If he's taking his time, that means his first thought isn't to give up.*

Was that logical? If not, it still made sense to me.

In the meantime, I was going crazy, and I had such an empty feeling. The way I interpreted losing him was in the form of a lover and a friend. Gradually, it seemed that I would end up losing a lover and a friend. To me, separation was going to be my only choice to protect what was left of my heart.

He once told me, "It doesn't have to be easy to be done."

I didn't want to see him anywhere with anyone, especially knowing that he wasn't mine, but I did want to see him at the same time. On the other hand, I thought I'd make an excuse to see him. I thought, *I'll get him a gift for Christmas, and then he'll have to see me.*

I didn't do it in the hope that we'd be together; I wanted to show him how much I cared for him, despite everything. When I came home, I went to the mall with a close friend. She was shopping for her boyfriend, and I was shopping for him. As we were window shopping, I asked her opinion on just about everything. Then I asked her thoughts on my getting him something.

She said, "Telley, I don't see anything wrong with it, but I know you. Just don't do too much because you still don't know where you stand with him. It's a thoughtful gesture, though."

I thought that was a reasonable and sensible answer. I ended up purchasing a green sweater, a gray-and-teal scarf, lip balm from Bath & Body Works, and a little massage thingy. I wanted to get more, but she stopped me. I can be very giving when I want to be, but not everyone deserves to be truly spoiled by me.

He finally got back to me—and said he wanted to just be *friends.*

I found this odd because I knew that wasn't what he really wanted. He was just scared and playing it safe. I knew this because although he said that, we were, again, still talking regularly.

Boy, please, I thought. *I run this.*

I knew that I couldn't keep putting myself out there and getting nothing in return. I was hurting myself, and though I wasn't expecting it, it was only a matter of time before everything would blow up in my face.

Remember: It's all about the effort on both ends.

Although Christmas always had been my favorite holiday, ever since my grandma passed away, it hadn't felt the same to me. It brought a lot of bittersweet emotions and wishful thinking: *I know with everything in me that this will be the year for me to finally have the love I'm missing, for me to finally fill that void. I just know I'm going to have a boyfriend around Christmas time, and that will do it for me.*

Yet again, it didn't.

It didn't because it never could. It never can.

I've since then grasped that absolutely nothing and no one will ever be able to fill that astronomical space. Nothing and no one will ever replace my grandma's love, my grandma's sweet face …

How foolish was I.

Christmas came and went, and I felt that same heavy strain brought by lingering pain. I reached out to him on Christmas (even though I said wouldn't), and it was very brief, as I'd expected, I guess. I didn't necessarily want a long conversation because we were "friends," and I didn't want to get excited by speaking to him either, so I left it at that.

The next thing I knew, we were planning to pop champagne for the New Year. I went to church that night, and when service ended, I came home and—like an idiot—I drunkenly called him. I asked him where he was and if he was going to come over. He said no because he was at a party—with the usual people.

The next day, I felt stupid—but not really. I decided I would give him his gift and then wash my hands of him. Once again, I reached out, and we met at a local skating rink. I gave him his gift and told him not to open it until he got home. As I turned around to leave, he asked for a hug.

I thought, *A hug? You hug your friends?* I said, "Nope," and turned to leave.

He shied away like I was making a big deal about it. I knew what my touch meant to him, and that's why I said no, very sternly. I could see it all in his eyes and gestures that it was hard for him to be around me and hold his composure.

> *See, I'm a holy woman. I know what it's like to give life to a being without ever needing to press skin against another.*

> —Reyna Biddy

I thought, *Aw, the little baby wants some good lovin', but that doesn't come for free, sir. I need that commitment and that security guaranteed. If I give it to you, my love, it's not going to be half-assed. My love runs through and through.* But he clearly knew nothing about that.

Maybe you got what I'm missin', would you keep it real if

My heart belonged to you, baby would you act right could
you be the one on my side or would you run and hide

If I gave my all to you, baby would you play
your part if I gave you my heart.

—August Alsina

Sunday, January 4, 2015

He called me on this Sunday evening, asking for a "date night." At first I was skeptical, and I had a right to be because he'd been playing with my emotions. I wondered what the difference was between his taking me out for dinner and his taking out one of his friends.

I said, "So you want to go to dinner with me, and we're just friends, right? Do you take all your friends out like this? Because this feels like a tad bit more."

Although we'd had a couple of these date nights previously, this was different—and he knew that—because he had chosen to friend-zone me. My plan was to go, get a free meal (even though I barely ate), and emphasize the fact that we were just friends. Even so, I was slightly hoping that when he saw me, he'd change his mind about us.

I wore a gray sweater-dress with black booties and my favorite bombshell perfume from Victoria's Secret. I knew I had to look good—not that it was a hard task for me, but I wanted to make sure I did the most in the subtlest way possible.

When he picked me up, I got in the car with an attitude; I was standoffish because I obviously had mixed feelings about him. All I could think about was what my sister told me before I decided to go with him: *"You are making yourself too available to him, Chántelle, too available. Tell him no."*

Clearly, I'm stubborn, and I didn't listen to her. But now that had me thinking: *I really should have made him work for my presence! Now he knows he can get me whenever he wants to.*

A part of me felt like he was taking advantage—and I was letting him— just to see how long I would hang in there without making him take responsibility for his actions. I think he thought that I owed him. He told me once previously that, "It was my turn to play catch-up."

He complimented me on my perfume, but I let it pass. I thought, *But you want to just be my friend, right? Make up your mind.*

He tried to start a conversation, but I got irritated and became quiet. He noticed my mood, pulled the car over, and stopped. "What's wrong?" he asked.

"Nothing."

"Well, I'm not moving the car until you tell me," he said, "or you could go back home because I didn't ask you out to have an attitude."

"Nothing is wrong," I told him. "I'm chillin'. Let's go to wherever we are going, not that you put much thought into this, but I'm here, so let's make a move."

We ended up at Bonefish Grill in Crofton, Maryland. I was pleased but still on edge.

We sat down and started talking, and only then did I express my frustration with him. I didn't order anything but water because I had an uneasy feeling. I was anxious and confused about what his motives were with me, with us.

We got on the topic of his circle of friends. and he told me who his close friends were; amazingly, he didn't mention me! If my good mood wasn't ruined before, it was definitely demolished at that moment. I had no words, and I had to second-guess my decision to grace him with my presence.

During dinner he said something striking, and I didn't know how to take it: "I see how much you love and care for me, but I keep pushing you away."

Surprised, I agreed with him. "Exactly. Why do you keep pushing me away?"

He had no answer.

I thought, *I'm over it. As long you can sleep at night knowing that this time, I didn't push you away, then that's your business.*

> Don't you ever say I just walked away
>
> I will always want you
>
> I can't live a lie, running for my life
>
> I will always want you … I never meant to start a war
>
> I just wanted you to let me in.
>
> —Miley Cyrus, "Wrecking Ball"

A strong woman will automatically stop trying if she feels unwanted. She won't fix it or beg; she will just walk away.

Focus equals peace of mind.

Clearly, that dinner was over almost as soon as it started. He tried flirting with me the rest of that night, but I continued to brush it off.

When we got to the car after dinner, I knew I should be ready to go, but I didn't want to. My mind and body always were in a constant battle over him.

My heart is in my mind. I think this is why I am an artist.

—Mahira Khan

I thought he'd take me home from there, but when he started driving, he asked if I wanted to see *The Hunger Games* with him because, apparently, he "had no one to go with."

I knew that was BS, but I went. I played along, but I also made it clear that we were just friends. "So don't try to cuddle with me or hold my hand. You stay on your side, and I'll stay on mine."

When we got to the theater, it seemed he'd disregarded everything we'd agreed upon. We only held hands, but still, that's a "couples" thing to do, and we weren't a couple.

The signs were obvious that he was saying one thing but wanting another.

After the movie, when we were walking to his car, he kept calling my name from behind me in a sweet, surrendering tone. I ignored him—that is, until I heard him say, "I think I want to try."

I turned to face him. "Try what?"

"Try us. I think I want to give us a chance."

"Is that your way of asking me to be your girlfriend?"

He laughed and said yes.

This was what I had been waiting for—regardless of how it happened—for the past nine months, so of course, I was all the way there for it. In fact,

I was so *for it* that I overlooked the lack of sincerity, the lack of certainty, the lack of seriousness that I deserved as a queen.

Foolishly, I accepted.

Inside I was jumping for joy, but I also asked him if he was sure about this. I wanted him to want it; that was important to me. I didn't want him to be unhappy; I wanted both of us to be happy and content with the decision of being together.

I asked if he was sure while simultaneously trying to come to grips with what had just transpired here.

"Yes, I'm sure," he said.

"Okay!"

Although I was ecstatic, it almost felt unreal, and that scared me. My intuition was kicking me a bit harder than usual, but I blocked it. I just wanted this to finally happen.

> To my women with the utmost respect, intellect
> We often forget and neglect intuition can see
> through elusive intent, listen to it.

> —H.E.R., "Against Me"

The bottom line was that I could tell he was scared. He seemed hesitant when said he wanted to "try," and I felt that, but I still went with it.

I wanted it to be genuine.

I wanted him to be ready.

I wanted him, us, and love to be enough; I desperately wanted that. I was willing to take that risk, even though it might come to a detrimental fall.

No matter how good of a woman you are, you will never be good enough for a man who isn't ready.

Over the next few days, I felt uneasy. I was supposed to be happy because this was what I'd wanted so badly, but, sadly, I didn't feel as complete as I would've hoped. I told a few people about us. "Take things slow" was still my motto because I feared the worst happening.

We spent Monday night together. The original plan was to watch a movie, but he got on my nerves, as usual, so that idea got tossed. I wanted to interact with him more—or at least try. I'd never really faced it, but some things tainted his image for me, and that held me back from being 100 percent comfortable around him.

The slight thought that I might be settling held me back. Why didn't I feel whole?

At this point, our conversations rarely were productive. For instance, that night I brought up that he always chose to spend time with his friends instead of with me. Of course, as always, he had a quick rebuttal. Instead of hearing what I was saying and seeing where he fell short and where I was coming from, he had to give a reason, which wasn't even a real reason. This was how we communicated most of the time. It usually ended before it started. We would talk in circles, and I'd get fed up. I despised repeating myself.

At the end of the day, people make time for who and what they want to make time for—always.

Wednesday was skate night. I tried to do things with him that weren't the cliché couples' activities. I wanted to do things that would be a distinct memory—things that made me feel carefree and reminded me of my happy place.

Skate night was a fun time but very awkward, to be honest. It was the first time we were out as a "couple," I read too much into everything. But who was I kidding? That's like telling water not to be wet. I couldn't deny how out of place I felt.

Lovey-dovey couple? Nah. We were far from it. This wasn't what I'd imagined at all. God probably was laughing at me.

It was clear that I'd fallen for the illusion that when we were together, I'd be different, and we would be different together, but that wasn't the case. I sold myself a fairy tale; I guess as most young girls do with their first loves.

Yet I kept ignoring it because this was what I wanted, and this was who I wanted it with.

As the night wound down, we sat in his car and talked for nearly three hours—much like having a good old therapy session. At this point, that was kind of our ritual. We dived straight into the meat of things when we start talking.

"So tell me about all the girls that you talked to while we weren't talking in college and high school!" I said. I have a bad habit of asking questions for which I really don't want the answer.

"No."

"Why?"

"Because that isn't going to help *us*," he said.

"But I want to know."

"I understand that you *want* to know, but if it isn't going to benefit what we're trying to do, then there is no need to dwell on it."

And just like that, I let it go, even though I was thinking, *Damn, it was that bad that you don't want to tell me?*

But it didn't matter. He was right—at least this time. The only thing that mattered was that I was there. He was there. We were there. And we were working toward the infamous *something*!

As we sat there, we listened to one of our songs, "Share My Life" by Kem.

And other endless slow food, it was a vibe.

The only real thing out there is love, everything else is an illusion.

—Keke Palmer

He lay on my chest with his arms wrapped around my tummy. I held him close like the little baby he was to me. It was a freeing moment, and we didn't have too many of them, so I cherished him and that time. The power of body language is very persuasive.

When soul mates unite (or reunite), there is always a pull of attraction that isn't just physical. This pull is their bodies' way of communicating to each other: *I love you. I breathe you. My heart yearns for every inch of you. We were always made for one another, and we realize it more and more as time goes on.*

You never miss a beat. Never.

Yet the bittersweet thing about that synchronization is that you quickly sense when things aren't right. You sense catastrophe among temporary comfort.

As we were talking, his mom called him.

I'd never met his family. Now that we were "official," it bothered me even more. I didn't know how he couldn't see that.

Based on the responses he was giving to his mom, she was asking general "mommy" questions. The next thing I knew, I heard him say, "I'm with my *friend* Chántelle."

In my head I screamed, *We ain't just* friends*!*

Obviously, I didn't say anything.

When they hung up, he read my body language.

Granted, we were true friends, but it wasn't just that. I rolled my eyes and mugged him so hard. Like, *Yeah, okay, I got ya, friend!* It felt like he was keeping me a secret from the important people in his life, and that really hurt; it still does.

But life goes on.

He said afterward that he planned on telling his mother about us. Part of me knew he wouldn't, but part of me settled for that. What a fool I was!

By 2:30 a.m., I said I had to go, so we said our goodbyes.

That Friday, January 9, I was out and about, when I got a call from a close friend. She said he'd called her that day.

Let's just say that a woman's intuition is everything.

She said that apparently, he didn't feel like he was in a relationship. He didn't feel the "butterflies," and he just didn't feel like he "was supposed to feel" when he was with me.

I thought, *What the hell are you talking about, sir?*

Yet when she told me this, my heart dropped. She said that she'd told him she didn't understand what this specific "feeling" was that he was looking for, and basing the value of a relationship on the temporary feeling of being "in love" or having "butterflies" all the time wasn't realistic.

Love is not all about the butterflies. It's also about the pain, work, and tears you face when taking on the shared responsibility of another's heart.

This—done genuinely, not flawlessly—creates your bond and builds power within a couple, feeding from that durable, soulful foundation.

I was beyond flabbergasted by what my friend was telling me. I wasn't thinking straight, but her information confirmed the feeling I had— that he was hiding his uncertainties from me. I was disoriented and felt distorted; and I just didn't understand. The minor doubts I'd had grew larger and larger.

It is the worst situation when the feelings you have for someone aren't mutual.

I thought, *Now we go to other people when we aren't feeling one another?* (The friend who called me was our mutual friend, but still …) *Is he saying all of this because of the distance? Where is this coming from? Is he going to give it up before it even starts?*

It hurt me to even think about it.

I couldn't eat.

I couldn't sleep.

I picked up very quickly that he was acting strange, distant, and overly sensitive about things I said after that. It was almost as if he was looking for a reason to argue, just to cut me off. I dreaded hearing, "Yeah, look, this isn't going to work, Chántelle."

When he finally expressed his uncertainty to me, I was in the grocery store with some friends. He called, and I dived right in.

"Are you okay with us being together?" I asked. "Are you sure you will be able to put 100 percent into us? Are you happy? Is this what you want as well?"

I understand being selfless and thoughtful of another's feelings, but I was giving him the opportunity to tell me that he wasn't happy. If this wasn't what he wanted, then he should have said so. The truth would come out eventually.

But he chose not to acknowledge anything. So then I had an issue with him. I didn't have respect for that at all. Because although it would wound me physically, mentally, and emotionally, it would hurt even more and be even more damaging if we stayed together when he didn't really want to be together.

He blathered on, giving me his BS. "I don't know. With this decision, I'm unsure, and usually when I make decisions, it's black or white. It's either a solid yes or no."

"What am I supposed to do with this information?"

And again, the conversation was left up in the air.

Looking back, that really should've been it for me. Yet I kept riding it out because I thought fighting, correcting my wrongs, and showing him that I wasn't a terrible person who'd give up on him was the answer.

But I got to a point when I asked myself, *which is best—to cut him or continue being patient with him?* My thoughts ate at me relentlessly.

Meanwhile, I was still strolling around the local grocery store, but I was so deep in that pointless conversation that I'd lost everyone that I'd come with. And I wasn't sure I'd bought what I needed—I wasn't focused on anything but him.

But at that point, it seemed that my entire world stopped. I can admit I was out of touch with reality. I was wrapped up in what he was thinking and what he was doing when he was alone or with his friends. It was a lot, and I drove myself insane, trying to anticipate his next move, his next word, his next breath.

What is he going to use as an excuse this time as to why we are not working? I asked myself that question one too many times.

The funny but necessary thing about God is that when you don't step aside and let him be God, he will move you and show you he is God!

There have been only a few times when I've felt I couldn't carry on: December 8, 2008, when my grandma passed (rest easy, Grandma), and January 10, 2015, my first heartbreak.

January 10—that day and time of truth came more quickly than I imagined. It was the day when I thought the entire world was crashing down, the day that tore and shattered my heart into pieces. It was the day I came face-to-face with a vicious and gruesome kind of pain that I never knew existed or believed was possible to feel.

It started off as a normal winter day in Philly. Although the wind was very harsh that day, it wasn't too out of the ordinary. I woke up that morning, disheveled (which had become my norm) from the night before.

> Always remember: Every emotion serves its purpose at its
> given time in your life. Never disregard it.

I just wasn't myself. The day went by, and inch by inch, second by second, I just kept feeling *off*. I was off. We were off. Everything involving energy was off.

He and I had small and pointless conversations throughout the day. I felt the tension, but I told myself, "You have to force this conversation with him about how awkward it's been. Do it tonight, when you're off work."

We had different agendas.

I wanted to have a conversation about how I'd been feeling lately, so I texted him: "What are you doing tonight?"

"I'm going out" was his text response.

More than likely with females, I thought, and that made my blood boil.

162

I texted, "Mmmm-kay, don't let your apparent 'anonymous feelings' make you conveniently forget that you have a girlfriend or that you're in a relationship."

I received no response to that until four or five hours later.

Around 9:30 that night, he called me. I was quick to answer the phone, of course, because I thought the conversation would go in the opposite direction from where it went.

He started the conversation off wrong. He knew I was upset, but he took his time in calling me and didn't care how that made me feel.

"First of all," he began, "I didn't respond to your last text message initially because I was trying to compose myself and not go off on you. Second, I would never cheat on you or anyone I am with, no matter who I am around, because that's not what I do."

"Blah, blah, *blah*!" I said. "Sounds good."

All that went right through one ear and out the other, especially because I already felt like he was being more distant than ever before. So, it was screw him for real at that point. And then, it happened.

God has the power to show you who's God.

Always, all ways.

—Alex Elle

He said, "Yeah, Chántelle, I can't do this. I realize that I can't give you what you want. I can't give you what you need. I realize that I'm only happy with you when you're happy, but when you're not happy, it's just too much for me. I'm sorry if you feel like I didn't give the effort or try like I said I would. I was being immature and a little boy when I made you feel that this is what I wanted. I led you on for my personal pleasure when this whole time I've been unsure.

"Now I'm sure that this *isn't* what I want. I made a mistake. I also know you said that if I'm not here with you at your worst, then I can't have you at your best. I will eventually end up regretting it, but that's a risk I'm willing to take. I would also suggest that you take time to yourself for about a year, not talking to anyone, just to soul search. If, at any time, you're open to being friends, I'm open to it. Obviously not now, but whenever you're ready. I really do care about you, and I love you."

I was frozen. Shocked. Numb. Speechless. Breathless. And I instantly felt *lifeless*.

I wouldn't wish that feeling on anyone. To have an internal open wound is the absolute worst pain anyone can experience, in my opinion.

I faintly responded with what I had left in me after he had ripped out my heart. I said, "I don't understand where this is coming from. I'm hurt, but I'm not going to cry. If this is what you want, then at this point, what can I do? I really hope you find what you're looking for. Be safe."

No less than a minute later, I called my older sister, and before I could get it all out, I broke down crying. I was surprised at my own reaction; I hadn't seen myself breaking down like that. I didn't foresee myself becoming the epitome of emotional damage. He didn't cheat on me. Isn't that the worst kind of pain? Isn't that pain much more sensible, rational, and valid to deem as "heartbreaking"?

Some expressed the opinion that what I'd experienced wasn't "that serious." To them, I say, "You're not *that serious* for attempting to discredit my feelings! Maybe you thought that the less harsh words he used helped ease that big pill to swallow, but it didn't."

As a matter fact, I would have preferred a big argument. Then I'd have known he was angry or that he hated me; then I've have known that I was absolutely and positively nothing to him. It would've helped me move on a lot more quickly. It would've made my skin with regard to him a lot thicker.

Yet he left this open-ended … and, surprisingly, that cut deeper.

I see pain as pain. There isn't a "greater" pain, especially when I'm emotionally invested. I still endured betrayal, humiliation, disloyalty, and deception to an extent. I still broke—and that hit me hard.

It was suffocating. It was violating. It was excruciating.

No joke.

I didn't know what to do with myself; emotionally, I was in deep, dark space. I was depressed but never talked to anyone about it. I endured this mostly alone, mostly by choice. I didn't want to feel this in the first place, so I definitely didn't want to place it on someone else.

I decided I'd write instead. I'd write dark, solemn pieces all the time to relieve what was on my heart.

Me loving you benefits no one.

I don't see how this yearning my heart has for yours still exists.

Loving you is only hurting me. Hurting me with what couldn't be.

Me loving you doesn't faze you.

We don't speak, so how is this love even reaching you?

How do I get out of this bind?

This indirect but direct, conscious but unconscious
bind, where my heart clearly has its own mind, where
my heart has clearly invested so much time …

How?

Walking around all day, every day with your memory
weighing heavy on my heart and bold on my sleeve.

Praising God, thanking God, and begging him continuously for
your heart, mind, body, and soul in its entirety. Longing for the day
that we can be together forever in every shape, form, and way.

All this grief, hostility, and confusion, with not one care, concern, or regard
from him, this being who supposedly loved and cared for me so much.

And for two and a half years after that, we didn't really speak.

The one time we did, of course, I was the one who reached out. It was
three months later, in March, and I knew it was a mistake. Nothing came
from it but more disappointment in his lack of care and concern for my
heart and spirit.

I thought, *You couldn't even check to see if I was alive? And then when I reach
out to you, you're short and brief with your replies, as if I did something to
you. Yes, I'm taking it personally. How do I believe a word that comes from
your mouth after that? How?*

Were we strangers or soul mates? The next two years were tough. My first
love and my first heartbreak, all in one, was a lot to take in.

I told myself every day, *Thank God we didn't have sex.* Because contrary to
what many believe, sex is meaningful and enhances emotional bonds and
attachments, consciously and unconsciously.

So if that had happened, I probably would've felt like driving home that
night to kill him.

Yet despite that, all this time had passed, and I still wasn't over him. I still
worried about him. I still cared for his well-being. I was consumed with
all that he was.

Simultaneously, however, I had so much animosity in my heart toward him that I wanted him to feel how I felt. I prayed often that someone would come along and sweep me off my feet, just so I could be distracted *and* be petty and make him jealous—make him see what he lost, what he missed out on, what he could now never have because he gave up on me.

That never happened, though, and I felt like I had taken five steps forward to get drop-kicked a hundred steps back. So I prayed. I prayed, and I prayed, and I prayed for this feeling to just leave me. The focus of my prayers started to shift from blaming and shaming, to seeking consistent serenity of mind, body, and soul. I reached a point where, although praying for him was second nature for me, I questioned if I should still do it because it seemed he was fine without me.

This was my daily prayer:

"I don't know what is happening, God, but I know that I truly love this idiot. All my intentions were good, and if we are never going to be anything in the future, and this is your way of telling me, then I pray all feelings and memories leave my mind so I can be at peace. In Jesus's name I pray, amen."

Every night, I got on my knees and essentially prayed the same prayer— after bawling my eyes out because that's how deep my wounds were. I just wanted it to be—either I have him, or I'm rid of him.

In the interim, I avoided social anything—social media, social outings— when I wasn't in Philly, all to lessen the chances of encountering something or someone that triggered a memory of *him*.

And I thought, *How can you pretend like you know what is real in public but can't realize it when it's right in front of your face? How does that work? How are you the victim here? How could your words and actions be so contradictory?*

It made no sense.

I wanted to ask *why* so badly, but distress and discomfort wouldn't let me. I couldn't get past the fact that people would look at us and not know anything or know only the half of our story.

I made an internal declaration: *I won't stand for being labeled the "evildoer" or an insensitive, irrational, and/or unstable crazy person that some have made me out to be.*

People may talk so negatively about you and build a certain image of you, based on your past, that even though you know yourself, you still settle for the shallow image they create of you.

That was me. I owed it to myself—I owed it to my soul—to speak up and clear the air on my name and character. It wasn't my concern whether what I said changed people's view of me, but I felt it was (and is) my duty to live in my truth and to continue to rise above all that tried to claim me in vain. It was my responsibility to wake up and give life back to that happy little girl who loved to play with Bratz dolls, and watched Oprah with her grandma and got on her nerves every day after school.

It was *her*—that girl, right there—who was—is—on her way to living life in full, all over again ... *like she never left.*

CHAPTER 14

The Outcome

God's Timing

God knows what you need, when you need it, where you
need it, why you need it, and how much of it you need.

My healing and sanity were the only things that I had left to depend on.
I was determined that I wasn't going to lose that too. Instead, I decided to
gather my pieces and meticulously learn about me—and I'm still learning.

Take your broken heart; make it into art.

—Princess Leia

Sometimes I wonder why we always seek an outcome. For me, it's because
if I put something out into the universe, I want to see a return on that
almost instantly.

That could be the millennial in me, always seeking that instant
gratification. But I'm learning over and over, day by day, that some of the
most rewarding outcomes are birthed from patience. They're birthed from
never knowing but always trusting it will be okay, or better yet, from not
expecting an outcome at all.

I'm realizing that the most meaningful and effective gestures are to force absolutely nothing.

Nothing.

That's a challenge for me.

To move with my heart, as if I don't fear it will fall apart, is beyond hard, but it's necessary. I always feel like I need to do something, like I didn't get an outcome that I wanted because I didn't *try* hard enough.

But my experiences have unveiled the beauty and serenity in not doing so much, in not forcing.

This realization has even brought me to question my complacency within trying so hard. That's the quickest way to burn me out.

I ask myself, *What if, this whole time, I've kept myself complacent because of my fixation on persistently "trying"?*

Sometimes not trying *is* trying.

What if I've received the opposite of my desired outcomes from always predicting, assuming, and acting on the idea of what I thought it should be because I was in my own way?

What the heck?

Yes, I'm a genius.

In the past, I've equated *not trying* with giving up, but now it's becoming clear that that's not necessarily what it means. In fact, most of the time that's not the case at all. What is and what is supposed to be comes naturally, my darlings.

It's not necessarily without *any* effort whatsoever but without any *added* effort, with the motive and intention behind it that "this has to work *exactly* like this."

That's a lot of weight on the powers that be. And they don't work well under pressure, so let it be.

What if, by my obsession with trying, I've hindered my own growth? My own progression?

It seems that that's definitely what I've done on so many occasions, especially the one I've just described. I've questioned my adequacy so many times when it comes to a love life and a writer's life.

Is this who I'm supposed to be with?

Am I enough?

Am I too much?

Am I really a writer, or is this going to blatantly suck?

The scary and unfortunate part is that I don't know the outcome for any of that. I just know it will be what it will be. Lo que sera, sera. I will be what I will be, for whoever needs me and my work. The infamous *it* will come to fruition eventually.

And I can learn from it all.

I just want to be in a space (if I can help it) where what I'm putting out is appreciated and reciprocated.

I deserve at least that. And so do you.

And as far as that other situation goes … well, it's all love.

We love people, and there's nothing we can do about that. Yet I've realized—through prayer, experiences, tears, and laughs—that the strength that I needed him to have emotionally wasn't there and still isn't. Maybe it never will be. Or maybe it will be eventually … but only time will tell. I know what I deserve, and I need my effort matched.

I can't discredit or waste this time that God is allowing me to become more in tune with myself, with my soul, with my heart's melody. I can't pass up getting to know myself in a more intricate, intimate, and essential way. I was never defined by my past, and neither are you.

I'm truly sorry that some can't see the heaven in me, see all that glows in me, and that they can't navigate my profound personality. I'm sorry they've failed to see all that was fruitful within me. Regardless, my light will shine brightly.

I'm just as lost as you may be, and that's why I wrote this. I don't know what the future holds, but I do know that love is greater than this world. The radiance of real love is intertwined within earth's synergy and is embedded in each of our beings.

And nothing and no one can stop that.

God is love.

I don't know why our hearts don't do what our minds tell them to do, but maybe that's the point of it all.

Perhaps it's the enticement of that mystery and the unknown and powerful correlation that brings us to an indescribable state of bliss, created through the laws of attraction from our own souls first, and then from another. Maybe this is what we've unconsciously always longed for.

We'll find out soon enough.

In the meantime, in between time, don't try, just do. Don't look for too much of a permanent outcome. Just let life happen because it's in divine order.

Don't stress over what you can't control. And be selective with what you can control.

Don't expect too much. Just *be*. Just happen. Just reasonably work, wait, and then see. Just be honest.

tell the truth.

to yourself first and to the children.

live in the present. don't deny the past.

live in the present and know the charge on you is to make this country more than it is today.

—Maya Angelou

i've burned all my masks.

i am—i stand before you here—naked.

draped and dripping in gold is the purest form of my soul.

here for you, is my raw story untold.

This is my truth.

Acknowledgments

This book is a dedication to self-love and vulnerability in its most free and fearless form. I thank God—I thank him first and foremost because I'd be nothing without him. I love him more than anything: thank you for my talents, for my vision, and for meticulously picking the tribe which surrounds me.

To my parents, thank you for always loving me and supporting me with whatever, no matter how crazy it may seem to you. Thank you for being my rock-my solid foundation and teaching me how to be strong and how to flourish in this world. I pray I make you proud every day to call me your daughter. You are my hope, my rhyme and reason, thank you for not changing on me like the seasons. I'm so glad you both are my parents, I wouldn't be as phenomenal without the balance that is the two of you.

To my sister, thank you for being my true best friend, for always getting the inside jokes, and for being love, a true confidant and for never judging me no matter what. Thank you for being there when you didn't have or want to and for being there just because sharing space feels good, feels normal, feels comforting, and feels like home. I love you.

To my aunt, thank you for always giving me legal and logical advice throughout this process and in general. To my high school counselor and confidant, who has counseled me through a lot and has seen me shed tears like no other, I love you so much and you are so very special to me. To my friends and extended family, thank you *so* much for it all. You have made a lasting impact and imprint on my heart, you have helped shape the woman I am and your experiences are unforgettable.

A special thank you to my cousin, who has helped me every step of the way with every inch of my life and brand. I love you Juice, and I can never repay you.

Thank you to my iHeartMedia family and to my best and close friend(s) (who are my family as well)—you know exactly who you are. We have been through a lot and if it weren't real we would've folded. Thank you for being true to your words. Thank you for the uncontrollable laughter and the genuine concerns. Each of you reflect me in a different way. I see the light in each of you, and I appreciate you all listening to me (as crazy and indecisive as I can be), for accepting me in my entirety, for correcting me when I'm wrong, for being there for me the best way you knew how and for always giving me sound advice with unconditional love and understanding attached to it.

To iUniverse, REC Philly and my entire creative team (you know who you are), thank you so much for your patience and for your willingness to work with me to bring unpleasant pieces of me to the light. To any and everyone else reading, whether you know me or not, thank you for believing in me and for trusting me enough to evoke deep, pure, and true emotions inside of you. I hope this memoir is what you needed to get through. I truly, truly love you.

To my ancestors, and to my angels: thank you for paving the way and for instilling fruitful seeds within me. I hope my work pleases you. I would be lost without you, and that's how I know you are still so very present. Thank you for your guidance and for loving, carrying, and watching over me and my family, despite everything.

Thank you for never giving up on me and seeing me before I could.

Finally, I want to thank myself for the continuous drive to move forward. For defeating my mind, for taking the time to cling to what's mine and to unpack and identify triggers that had a hold on my beautiful mind. For realizing my beauty derives beyond skin deep. For loving and seeing myself through. For being the ultimate example of self-love for me now and the younger me too. For fulfilling the promises, I made to myself and holding myself accountable. For being brave enough to say what I have to say in the most vulnerable way. For being able to humble myself and realize that my existence is greater than me. For acknowledging my imperfections and being able to still stand, to still rise, and to rise higher, even after the great fall.

This is a celebration for you. I love and value you more than ever—my skin, my mind, my soul etc. I will always fight for YOU.

I still have much to learn on this journey but there's no other place I'd rather be than with me. This is the definition free.

This is for you, enjoy this moment.

Love, Self.

CPSIA information can be obtained
at www.ICGtesting.com
Printed in the USA
LVHW111735131119
637254LV00003B/113/P